WHEN YOU DON'T KNOW WHERE YOU'RE GOING YOU CAN NEVER GET LOST.

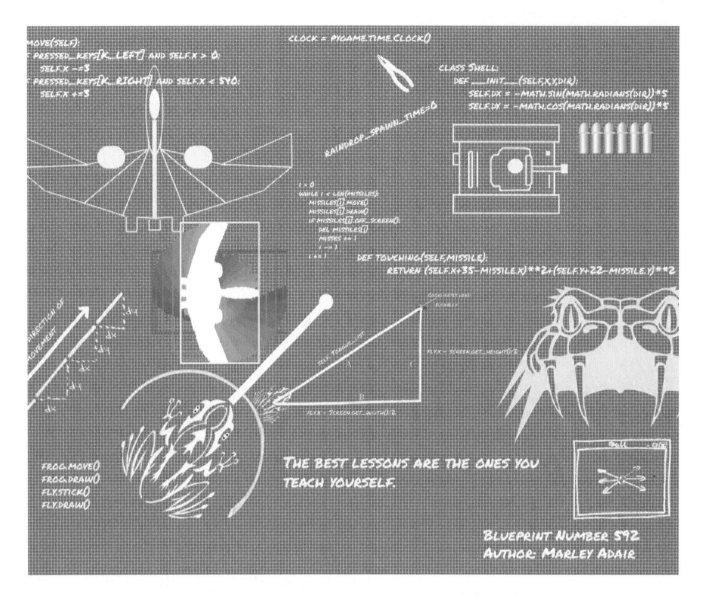

THE BEST LESSONS ARE THE ONES YOU TEACH YOURSELF.

BLUEPRINT NUMBER 592
AUTHOR: MARLEY ADAIR

BY THE TIME YOU'VE FINISHED THIS BOOK YOU'LL BE ABLE TO...

- BUILD CLOUDS WITH FALLING RAIN AND AN UMBRELLA TO KEEP OFF THE RAIN.

- BUILD SPACE INVADERS WITH RANDOMLY ATTACKING INVADERS.

- BUILD PONG WITH A HIT FUNCTION THAT ACCELERATES THE BALL.

- BUILD A ROTATING FROG WITH AN EXTENDING TONGUE THAT CATCHES FLIES OR STARVES TO DEATH IF IT DOESN'T.

- BUILD A TANK BATTLE GAME WITH MOVING OBSTACLES, SHELLS THAT BOUNCE AND AMMUNITION THAT RUNS OUT BUT CAN BE REPLENISHED AT AN AMMO DUMP.

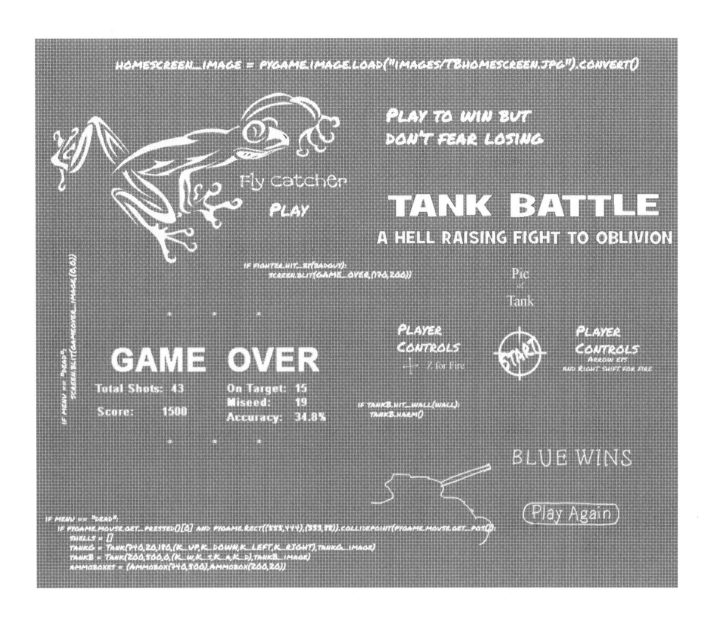

You'll also know how to build Start Up screens, Game Over screens, Health Bars, Scores, Sound Effects and various other common gaming techniques.

And you'll be familiar with Classes, Loops, Functions, Iteration and a whole bunch of other programming skills that are the basis for becoming a software engineer.

Good Luck

www.python-hunting.com

Contents

Chapter 3 The rain factory

Chapter 4 Where we get arty

Chapter 5 Where we meet the bad guys

WOAH!

I FEEL LIKE THIS HAS
HAPPENED BEFORE

Chapter zero

The tedious bit at the beginning...

Python

The first thing to do is install Python on your computer. Rather than describe this process here, we suggest you google **installing Python.** There are many online guides and youtube videos.

How-To Geek has good guide at:

https://www.howtogeek.com/197947/how-to-install-python-on-windows/

It helps if all your updates are installed.

The code in this book works with both Python 2 and Python 3. The two versions are very slightly different. The current version of Python 3 is 3.6.1 and you're probably best going with that.

Macs come with Python already installed.

Pretty much all versions of **Linux** come with Python pre-installed.

If you want to check your computer has a version of Python installed you can open a command line (see page 3) and type: **python** and press return. If you have Python installed then you get a few lines telling you which version you have. If not, you'll get an error.

WHAT IS THIS PLACE?

I DON'T KNOW.

Pygame

You will also need to install Pygame. Pygame is a set of modules that allow you to make games in the Python language. Using Pygame is the most fun you can have while learning Python.

We're going to use **pip**. **Pip** is a program that allows you to easily download and install libraries that go with Python. A library is kind of like an add on.

On **Windows** go to:

https://bootstrap.pypa.io/get-pip.py

Depending on your browser either you'll be asked if you want to open with python, in which case go right ahead and do that. This will install **pip**.

Or you'll have to save to your desktop (or anywhere you want) and then right click the icon, select **Open With** and then choose **Python**. This will install **pip**. You can then delete from your desktop.

Now open a command line. To do this, hit the windows icon bottom left. Type **cmd** into *Search*, and click on **cmd** under programs. A command line will open. There, type in:

python -m pip install pygame

Hit return and **pygame** will be installed on your computer.

When this book was first published we told people to install Pygame by doing the following:

Head to the **pygame.org** website and click on downloads. You'll find a list of download options. Pick the one that matches your version of Python. It will automatically install in the correct place.

This might still work, but **pip** has been introduced to make installing python libraries easier so it's probably best to use it.

On a **Mac** you need to open a terminal (see page 3) and type:

sudo easy_install pip

Hit return. Things will happen. (It might prompt you for your regular password.) This installs **pip**.

Then type:

sudo pip install pygame

Hit return. Pygame should be installed.

For **Linux**

Given the many varieties of Linux, you're going to have to look up instructions for you distro. You need to install pip, or pip3 if you're using python 3.

Then type the following into a terminal and hit return:

sudo pip install pygame

Or **sudo pip3 install pygame** if you're using python 3.

And pygame should install.

WHAT'S THAT?

LOOKS LIKE A LAPTOP COMPUTER. IT HAS FIVE PICTURES OF YOU AND ME STUCK TO THE CASE. HOW WEIRD.

Throughout this book we've placed sections of code in boxes.

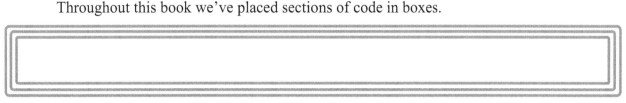

The triple boxes contain a complete code for what we're trying to do.

The grey boxes contain one or a few lines that deal with a specific task. They usually come with an explanation underneath.

The complete code quickly grows to become too much to fit on a single page of this book. We have put complete copies of the code in an appendix at the back of the book. However, on the website, in the code tab, there is a version of the code complete to a particular page in the book. For example, if you are on page 71, where we talk about while loops, you can go to the website and see a working copy of the code so far, with the while loop highlighted. This can help if you're not sure exactly in what order the sections of code go or how they are indented.

The first part of the book is given to falling rain and a space invaders game. We introduce many topics, such as classes, functions, loops and the like. The second part of the book takes what we've learned and applies it to building a pong type game, a flycatcher game and a tank battle. You can see and play all the games on the website. By the end you should understand the basic techniques to build 2D shoot em up type games as well as ball games. Using some imagination you'll be able to make other types of games. You'll also have learnt many techniques used for all programming in Python.

We are already working on a second book that will use a platformer game to introduce some more advanced programming techniques.

IDE vs a text editor

Integrated development environments (IDEs) are software applications that aid your programming. Eclipse is a popular multi-language IDE. If you use one it will have debugging tools, intelligent code completion and the like. And as you develop as a programmer they have more useful stuff.

Many programmers just use a regular text editor. A text editor will number your lines, which is useful, and color code some parts of your programs. Some have a few other tools. But for the most part you're left on your own.

Some people find IDEs annoying to use, others swear by them. Marley, who is the proper programmer of the two authors of this book, uses a text editor. Brian, who is more of a teacher than a programmer, would also suggest using a text editor at first. Notepad++ for Windows or geddit on Linux, or Atom or Emacs for anywhere are plenty good enough.

There are, no doubt, many programmers and teachers who would disagree, though we suspect the majority would suggest starting with with a text editor. If you're going to use an IDE then we would recommend a more basic type like WingIDE. Maybe once you get the hang of one of these you could move on to Eclipse. IDEs have their own learning curve. We suggest you don't use an IDE called Idle as pygame doesn't work so well with it.

I THINK I UNDERSTAND SOME OF THIS CODE. I DON'T KNOW HOW. IT'S LIKE I'VE SEEN IT BEFORE SOMEWHERE.

I FEEL LIKE I WAS JUST DOING SOMETHING IMPORTANT. AND THEN I WAS HERE. I WAS WITH SOME ONE. WE WERE... I DON'T KNOW. I CAN'T REMEMBER A THING.

Typing

We think it's important you actually type in the code. Copying and pasting code from a website won't make you a programmer any more than copying and pasting a picture from the net will make you an artist.

Although the code is on the website, this is just to enable you to see the complete code and help you follow it. You won't be able to cut and paste from it. Sorry.

Indents, tabs and spaces

In Python indents mean something. We talk more about this in chapter one but for now you might find it useful to set your tab key to insert 4 spaces. It is normal when indenting to use four spaces. Python doesn't actually insist on this, so long a you always use the same number of indents Python doesn't mind. But use four.

In Notepad++ go to the **Preferences** under **Settings** and select tab settings. Click the **Replace by space** box, and set the tab size to 4. For other text editors and IDEs you'll have to work it out or Google how to do it.

Note. If you need to indent a section of code by four spaces you can block it all in and hit **tab**. If you hit **shift**+**tab** it will remove the four spaces. This only works if you've configured your tab key to place 4 spaces.

All those brackets

One of the obvious things to notice when you first look at a piece of code is the brackets. They're all over the place and it almost seems as if they're placed at random. Some bits of code have brackets around them and some don't. There are brackets with nothing inside and brackets with other brackets inside. Sometimes you see lines ending like this:)))

It won't be long until you get the bracket thing; it just takes some getting used to. It's important to know that brackets come in pairs. For every opening bracket there's a closing bracket.

Brackets are mostly used in one of two ways. They lump things together. Like this:

```
(thing,thing,thing)
```

Just one thing on its own doesn't usually need brackets:

```
thing
```

Or they go on the end of a function. A function in just something that does something. This is all explained in the main body of the book.

```
function()
```

Sometimes we put things in functions. Like this:

```
function((thing,thing)) or function((thing,thing),thing)
```

Sometimes Functions can go inside other functions. Like this:

```
function(function())
```

Or any combination of the above:

```
function(function((thing,thing)))
```

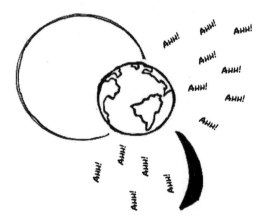

(An unbalanced parentheses will cause the earth to veer to the left, sending it crashing into the sun.

Colons

There are rules about where to use colons. If you miss a colon your program won't run. But don't worry about it. You'll get error messages to warn you where a colon is missing, and you'll soon get the hang of where to place them. Colons are placed at the end of any line that precedes an indent (page IV). There is an example in the pseudo code below.

Spelling

All the words used in Python are spelt in American English. For example "color". You have to use this spelling. Python wouldn't understand "colour".

The authors of this book, Brian and Marley, are English and Scottish. Therefore, for the text of the book, we've used British English with the exception of the word color, which we've spelt the American way throughout.

Pseudo code

Pseudo code is used to describe a computer program. It is structured like a computer program but is designed to be read by a human rather than a machine. Something like this:

```
IF THE RIGHT ARROW GETS PRESSED:
    TURN RIGHT
IF THE LEFT ARROW GETS PRESSED:
    TURN LEFT
```

We sometimes use pseudo code to show what's going on when it isn't obvious from the actual code. It won't work as real code; it's just to help people understand what's going on.

PYTHON WAS DEVELOPED BY A DUTCHMAN CALLED GUIDO
VAN ROSSUM. HE NAMED PYTHON AFTER THE BRITISH
COMEDY GROUP MONTY PYTHON. THE IDLE IDE WAS
NAMED AFTER ERIC IDLE, A MEMBER OF MONTY PYTHON.
VAN ROSSUM HAS BEEN GIVEN THE TITLE, "BENEVOLENT
DICTATOR FOR LIFE" BY THE PYTHON COMMUNITY FOR HIS
CONTINUED INPUT INTO THE LANGUAGE.

HOW DO YOU KNOW THIS?

READ IT IN A BOOK

To make a File –

Open Terminal
cd ella
cd Project folder name

make a new File
Touch myfile.pg

to run app

Python filename.py

Chapter One

pwd   shows current folder

cd ..   go back one folder

Creating the universe...

The big bang

WHAT'S THAT IN THE SKY
OVER THERE?

I DON'T KNOW. IT'S LIKE A BIG
ROUND THING. I WONDER HOW IT
GOT THERE.

```
import pygame, sys
from pygame.locals import *
pygame.init()
screen = pygame.display.set_mode((640,480))
while 1:
    for event in pygame.event.get():
        if event.type == pygame.QUIT:
            sys.exit()
    screen.fill((255,255,255))
    pygame.draw.circle(screen,(0,255,0),(100,150),20)
    pygame.display.update()
```

Open up whichever text editor or IDE you're using and type in the code from the box above. Then save the file, giving it a name and the extension **.py**. Something like **firstprogram.py** should do it. You should create a folder, called something like Python Stuff, to keep all your Python files in.

```
                        *C:\Users\Brian\firstprogram.py - Notepad++

 File  Edit  Search  View  Encoding  Language  Settings  Macro  Run  Plugins  Window  ?                    X

 firstprogram.py

    1   import pygame, sys
    2   from pygame.locals import *
    3   pygame.init()
    4   screen = pygame.display.set_mode((640,480))
    5   while 1:
    6       for event in pygame.event.get():
    7           if event.type == pygame.QUIT:
    8               sys.exit()
    9       screen.fill((255,0,0))
   10       pygame.draw.circle(screen,(0,255,0),(100,100),20)
   11       pygame.display.update()

 Python file length : 330   lines : 11        Ln : 11  Col : 28  Sel : 0 | 0         Dos\Windows    UTF-8 w/o BOM    INS
```

We're going to talk you through the code over the following pages.

Type in the code from page 1. The actual document will look something like the one above.

If your text editor shows up some colors don't worry about them; they're just there to make the code easier to read. They don't mean anything. To the left of the text there are line numbers, which can be useful, and some other symbols which you don't need to worry about.

The **indents** are important. Make sure the first five lines are all perfectly lined up. And the same for lines six, nine, ten and eleven. When indenting use four taps of the space bar. Don't use the tab button unless you've set it to insert spaces (see page -4). There is more about indenting on page 21.

Note there is a double equals sign on line 7. There's more about the difference.

THE GREAT THING ABOUT THE SUN IS THAT IT KEEPS AT THE PERFECT DISTANCE ALL THE TIME. NOT SO CLOSE IT BUGS YOU AND NOT SO FAR THAT IT LEAVES YOU COLD.

Run Run Run

Now we need to open a command or terminal line to run the code.

Windows

In Notepad++ you can do this by clicking in **File** then hovering over **Open Containing Folder** and clicking on **cmd** from the side menu.

Or from the search line in the start menu type **cmd** and hit return.

Mac

On a Mac open your Applications folder, then open the Utilities folder, then open the Terminal application.

Linux

If you're using Linux you'll be used to using a terminal. From a terminal use cd to find the directory where you've saved your file.

The command/terminal lines on all three systems look and behave in a similar way.

HEY, LET'S GO POKE THINGS
WITH A STICK.

YOU NOW WHAT I WAS SAYING ABOUT
THE SUN? A LOT OF PEOPLE COULD
LEARN FROM THAT.

Once we have a command line or terminal open, type in **python** followed by the **file name**.

We write "python" to let the system know we need Python to run the file.

Then we write the name of the file with its extension.

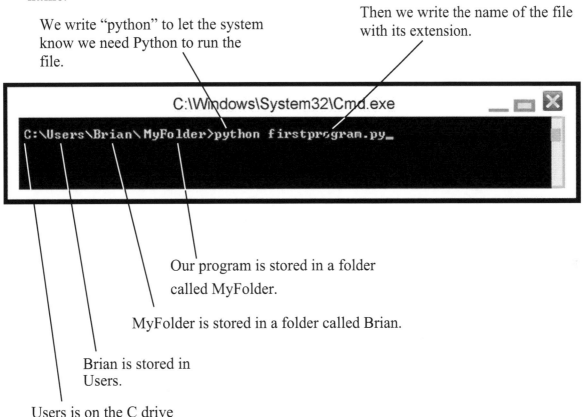

C:\Windows\System32\Cmd.exe

C:\Users\Brian\MyFolder>python firstprogram.py_

Our program is stored in a folder called MyFolder.

MyFolder is stored in a folder called Brian.

Brian is stored in Users.

Users is on the C drive

Hit the return and a window should appear on your screen. It's not that exciting but it's the first step to building a game. (Actually, it still excites me -Brian.)

THAT'S ALL IT TAKES TO CREATE THE UNIVERSE?

CREATING UNIVERSES IS EASY. THE TOUGH BIT IS MAKING THE STUFF THAT GOES IN THE UNIVERSE DO WHAT YOU WANT IT TO. JUST ASK GOD.

When Things Go Wrong

Sometimes things don't go quite as planned. The screen many not have appeared.

When we run a program in the command line and it doesn't work, the command line will tell us where the problem is. In the example below the problem is on the 6th line.

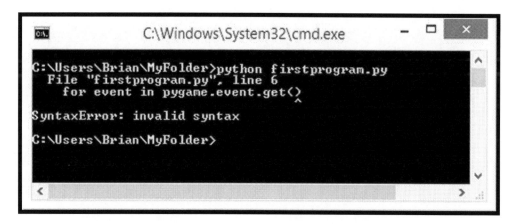

The most common errors when starting are syntax errors. This is when we get the grammar of the program wrong. We might have an indent problem, like we haven't always used four spaces for each indent. Or we might have missed a bracket. In the example above we've missed a colon. Whatever the problem, keep trying to figure it out. Because we are telling you what to write just now, almost all your errors will be typing errors. However, if you're already experimenting with the code then take a little time to try and figure out problems. Having the patience to do this is a major part of programming.

NOTHING'S GOING TO
GO WRONG. IF NOTHING GOES WRONG THEN

WE'RE NOT LEARNING ANYTHING.

A Toolbox

Now we'll go through each line in turn and see what it does.

```
import pygame, sys
```

The first line is us choosing our tools. When we fix a bike or cook a cake we need to use the right tools. The same goes for computer programming.

 **Pygame** is a box of tools used to make graphics for games and animations.

Sys allows Python to talk to the part of your computer that runs Python.

```
from pygame.locals import *
```

This line just sets up some of **Pygame**, making it easier to use later on.

```
pygame.init()
```

This line gets **Pygame** ready for use. You could say it turns **Pygame** on.

```
screen = pygame.display.set_mode((640,480))
```

Our universe is called **screen**. It is the place where everything in our game will happen.

There are two numbers in the brackets at the end of the line. The first, 640, is the width of the screen. The second, 480, is the height. Try changing them in your program to make the size and shape of your universe change.

When you make changes to your program make sure you remember to save them (Ctrl S, or Cmd S on a Mac) before running the program from the command line or terminal. Python runs the last <u>saved</u> version of your code. Forgetting to save can be frustrating.

I DON'T THINK THIS CAKE IS QUITE COOKED. DAMMIT. I FORGOT TO SAVE CHANGES AFTER I TOOK IT OUT THE OVEN.

Game Loop

```
while 1:
```

This is the beginning of the **game loop**. It's often called the **main loop** but we're going to call it the **game loop**. Everything before this line is getting things ready. Once we're in the loop things happen pretty fast. This part of the program repeats many times a second. It is where button presses and mouse clicks are detected. It's where anything moving on the screen is controlled, and stuff like collisions, scores and lives are kept track of. We'll be moving onto these subjects pretty soon.

For now note that after this line there are some indented lines. These indented lines will happen inside the **game loop**. That is, they get repeated many times a second.

Some programmers write:

```
While True:
```

It does exactly the same thing.

YOU'VE BUILT A ROBOT.
WHAT DOES IT DO?

IT BUILDS ROBOTS. ADDING LEGS.

ADDING TOUCH SENSORS.
ADDING AI UNIT.

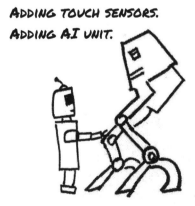

A Fast Exit

```
for event in pygame.event.get():
    if event.type == pygame.QUIT:
        sys.exit()
```

Once we are in that game loop we need to able to get out of it. These three lines are how we do it.

The first line detects anything that's happened during the last game loop, like a key being pressed or the mouse being moved.

The next line asks if one of those things was the  being clicked. In **Pygame** the red box with the cross in it is called QUIT.

The last line says if the ▨ was clicked on then let's close down this program.

It doesn't matter if you don't understand exactly what is going on here, but it is important to get these lines right. By the time you've finished this book you will understand what is going on here. Once your game is up and running these lines of code are you best way to exit. Not having them is like getting on a bus but having no way to get off -you're just going to keep going around in circles all day.

If this doesn't work you can go to your terminal and press `ctrl` + `c` or even just close your terminal or command line.

ADDING DEATH LASERS.
ADDING HUMAN
TARGETING SYSTEM.

CTRL C
CTRL C

9

Before we move on we're going to check out some technical terms.

== vs =

In Python you use = to give a value. If you write: b=2 you're saying make b equal to 2. It could have been something else before but now it's 2.

If we write b==2 we're usually asking if b is equal to 2. b could be anything. If could be 593. But it might be 2. Here we want to know if b is 2.

Functions

A function is something that does something. It might draw a circle or fill a screen or fetch some information.

All functions end with parenthesis; that is, a pair of curved brackets.

() ← Like this

The brackets sometimes have bits of information in them that the function uses, but even if there's no information we keep the brackets just to let everyone know we're dealing with a function.

In this book, when we talk about a function we're going to put the parenthesis on the end. We'll write, the move() function. We're doing this just to let you know we're talking about a function. Most programmers wouldn't do this.

Arguments

Arguments are the bits of information that go in the brackets.

Here's a function we're going to use later on:

clock.tick(60)

The function is the clock.tick() and the argument is the 60.

Clock.tick() knows it wants one argument and will look for it in those brackets. It knows it's going to get a single number. If you put a word or two numbers in the brackets it will get confused. But one number makes it smile and say, "I know what to do with that."

In this case it's making a clock that ticks 60 times a second.

(Clock.tick() can also take no argument. In this case it will return how fast your program is looping.)

Okay, let's get back to the program.

```
screen.fill((255,0,0))
```

Here we have a **screen.fill() function**. You can probably guess what it does.

The three numbers in the brackets represent a **color**. We talk about colors on the opposite page.

The **screen.fill() function** takes one **argument,** but the **argument** is made of three numbers. To let Python know that this is just one **argument** with three bits of information, we bind the numbers together in some brackets. This is why we have two sets of brackets here, one for the **function** and one for the **argument** in the function.

When we bind numbers together like this it's called a **tuple**. There is more about tuples on page 57.

The **(640,480)** in **pygame.display.set_mode((640,480))** is also a **tuple.**

So **screen.fill()** fills our screen with a color. This is the background on which we will place other objects.

HEY, LOOK. I JUST FILLED THE WORLD WITH A
BEAUTIFUL RED COLOR.

IT IS BEAUTIFUL. IT'S A SHAME THIS BOOK
IS PRINTED IN BLACK WHITE.

DAMN THE HIGH PRICE OF COLOR PRINTING. I BET
THE AUTHORS WOULD HAVE LOVED TO HAVE
PRINTED THIS BOOK IN COLOR.

color

color is always given using the **rgb** system. The three numbers in the parenthesis are how much red, green and blue are being mixed to give the final color. The amount of each color is set somewhere from 0 to 255. So in the color (255,0,0) we have 255 bits of red, and zero of green and blue. (0,0,0) would have no color and therefore be black. (255,255,255) makes white. (255,140,0) would give us a dark orange. There are plenty of places online the list all the colors. When mixing these colors we follow the rules for mixing light, not mixing paint.

Try messing around with different colors.

Note: If all three numbers are the same, like **(75,75,75)**, then you get a shade of grey. Silver (192,192,192) is a shade of grey.

Now let's look at the next line.

```
pygame.draw.circle(screen,(0,255,0),(100,150),20)
```

As you can see we have another function. Again, it's pretty obvious what it does.

pygame.draw.circle() is a function that takes four **arguments**. You have to give it those four arguments, and in the correct order, or it will get stroppy and refuse to behave. We'll go through each in turn. The actual function is **circle()**. It's in a sub-module called **draw. draw** is inside the **Pygame** module.

screen

The first argument is where the circle gets placed. It seems obvious that it would be placed on the screen but remember that **screen** is our name for what fills the display. A circle could be placed on other objects that are in turn placed on the screen. So the function has to know where to place the circle.

(0,255,0)

Here is the color of the circle. (Green in this case.)

(100,150)

This argument is the position of the circle on the screen. Position is given by a tuple containing two numbers. The first is the **x-position**. This is the distance in pixels of the centre of the circle from the left hand edge of the screen. The second value is the **y-position**. This is the distance of the centre of the circle from the top of the screen.

20

The final argument is the radius of the circle.

You have the option of putting in a fifth argument. This would be border width, giving you an empty circle. But if you don't put it in **Pygame** just solid fills the shape. Try putting it in. Just type a comma after the 20 and then a 5. Or a 1. Experiment.

The position argument, (340,280), marks the position of the centre of the circle. But if you draw a rectangle the position argument marks the the top left corner of the rectangle. Also, rather than having a separate argument for the size of the rectangle, it adds width and height onto the end of the position argument. So for rectangles the third argument will have four separate values, two for position and two for size.

Try it and see. Add in the line:

```
pygame.draw.rect(screen,(0,255,0),(100,100,40,30))
```

Place it after the **pygame.draw.circle()** line. Try putting different numbers into that third argument. And then try giving the circle and the rectangle the same position. And swap the lines around so the rect line comes before the circle line. Always remember to save the changes you make before running the program.

The **pygame.draw.rect()** function can also take an extra argument for border width on the end.

Showing off

```
pygame.display.update()
```

And finally the last line. This line takes all the screen changes that have happened in the **game loop** and pastes them onto the display in one go. Without this line, nothing you've done will ever be seen.

ONCE YOU CAN PUT A CIRCLE ON A SCREEN YOU CAN PRETTY MUCH DO ANYTHING. RIGHT?

SURE. IT'S LIKE ONCE YOU INVENT THE WHEEL, SPACE PROBES TO MARS AND PHONES THAT OFFER PSYCHOTHERAPY ARE INEVITABLE.

OO. I THINK I JUST PROGRAMMED THE SEA TO PLAY CRICKET.

Chapter Two

Where we get moving...

I like to move it

Add the highlighted lines to your program and see what happens.

```python
import pygame, sys
from pygame.locals import *
pygame.init()
screen = pygame.display.set_mode((640,480))
xpos = 50
while 1:
    for event in pygame.event.get():
        if event.type == QUIT:
            sys.exit()
    xpos += 1
    screen.fill((255,255,255))
    pygame.draw.circle(screen,(0,255,0),(xpos,200),20)
    pygame.display.update()
```

You might be wondering why the **screen.fill()** function is in the game loop? Why not just fill the screen once at the beginning and be done with it rather than do it every time?

Try putting it before the **while 1:** line. It won't need to be indented there.

HEY. WHAT'S UNDER
THE SCREEN FILL?

LEMMIE OUT OF HERE...

HELP..

17

Variables.

Remember this line?

`pygame.draw.circle(screen,(0,255,0),(340,280),20)`

And remember how the third argument controls where on the screen the circle is placed?

If we want something to move on the screen, we are going to have to change these numbers. But 340 is 340 and is always going to be 340. What we need is a number than can change.

What we need is a variable. We can just think of it as a number that can change. To create one we give it a name and we give it a value. For example:

Lives = 4

I have just created a variable called "Lives" and given it the value 4. The important thing is that the value 4 can change. I can write some code that says, if I die take 1 away from that 4. Make it a 3.

To move the circle we're going to create a variable called xpos, give it a value and then change that value to make it move.

Note: You might have noticed that we've already created some variables. Screen was created in the same way, using a = sign. A variable is really just a place where we store any data that can change.

MY PARENTS DIDN'T BELIEVE IS LABELLING THINGS. THEY SAID ONCE YOU NAME SOMETHING YOU DEFINE IT AND LIMIT IT.

WHAT DID THEY CALL YOU?

WHATEVER THEY FELT WAS APPROPRIATE AT THE TIME. FOR SOMEONE WITH NO NAME I HAD A LOT OF NAMES

```
xpos = 50
```

Here we have created a variable called **xpos** -this is short for **x-position**- and given it the value **50**. Although you can call a variable anything you like, it's a good idea to use names that relate to what the variable does. That way it is easier to find mistakes later on. It also makes it easier for other people reading your code to quickly understand what's going on.

This line is placed in the first section of the program, before the **game loop**. The **variable** is only created once so it doesn't need to be inside the loop.

```
pygame.draw.circle(screen,(0,255,0),(xpos,200),20)
```

The **draw.circle()** function now reads the x-position as **xpos**. But Python knows that xpos = 50 so it places the circle at the x-position 50.

```
xpos += 1
```

This line is in the game loop. It adds 1 to the value of **xpos** every time the loop goes around. So what's going to happen? The circle's x-position will change.

+=1 is just a quick way of adding one to a value. +=5 would add 5. - =2 would take away 2. *=3 would multiply it by three. And /=6 would divide by 6.

RUN, YOU BEAUTIFUL, CRAZY
CIRCLE, RUN LIKE THE WIND. BUT IT'S GOING TO GO OFF THE
EDGE OF THE SCREEN! WE NEED
TO STOP IT.

Taking control

To get some control we're going to remove the "xpos +=1" line and replace it with the highlighted lines. Run the program and press the right and left arrows on your keyboard.

```python
import pygame, sys
from pygame.locals import *
pygame.init()
screen = pygame.display.set_mode((640,480))
xpos = 50
while 1:
    for event in pygame.event.get():
        if event.type == QUIT:
            sys.exit()
        pressed_keys = pygame.key.get_pressed()
        if pressed_keys[K_RIGHT]:
            xpos += 1
        if pressed_keys[K_LEFT]:
            xpos -= 1
    screen.fill((255,255,255))
    pygame.draw.circle(screen,(0,255,0),(xpos,200),20)
    pygame.display.update()
```

BUT I WANT ALL MY CREATIONS
TO BE WILD AND FREE.

LET'S HOPE YOU DON'T WORK ON
DRIVERLESS CAR TECHNOLOGY.

Indents

Indents are important in Python. They're a way of splitting the code into chunks. When a line is indented it gets put into the same chunk as the line above.

As we said before, it is normal to use four taps of the space key to indent a line. (Setting the tab key to do this is explained on page -4.)

In pseudo code indents usually work some thing like this:

```
if the right arrow is pressed:
    move the spaceship to the right    } Chunk 1
if the space bar is pressed:
    lower the shields                  } Chunk 2
    fire the missile
```

Line 2 will only happen if Line 1 is true.

Similarly Lines 4 and 5 will only happen if Line 3 is true.

If a line isn't true, for example, if the right arrow isn't being pressed, then the program will ignore all the indented lines underneath and move on to the next line that's exactly underneath it.

As we can see from the Fast Exit code on page 6, it is possible to have chunks within chunks. In that example, line 2 will only be read if line 1 is true, And line 3 will only be read if line 2 is true.

Note: We place a colon at the end of a line that has indented lines after it.

```
pressed_keys = pygame.key.get_pressed()
```

pygame.key.get_pressed() creates a **list** of all the keys on the keyboard and whether they are pressed on not. We've then called this list **pressed_keys**. You'll notice that **pressed_keys** is also a variable. A **list** is another kind of **variable**.

We could have called the **list** anything we liked but it's conventional and sensible to use this name or something similar. Some programmers use the name **keys**. We will be seeing far more about creating and using **lists** later on.

```
if pressed_keys[K_RIGHT]:
    xpos += 1
```

The first line above checks though the list to see if the "**K_RIGHT**" key has been pressed. (Note: Those are square brackets. This is usual when dealing with lists.)

The "**K_RIGHT**" button is the right arrow on your keyboard.

The second line is what happens if the program discovers it is true that the "**K_RIGHT**" is being pressed. In this case it adds 1 to **xpos**.

In the program on page 20, you can see we also have a line detecting whether "**K_LEFT**" is being pressed, together with the command to reduce **xpos** by 1 should this turn out to be true.

You don't have to add or subtract 1. Try 2 or 10.

We are also going to add in a clock and a caption. Neither are essential but it's probably a good idea to get into the habit of adding the clock.

```
import pygame, sys
from pygame.locals import *
pygame.init()
pygame.display.set_caption("First Program")
screen = pygame.display.set_mode((640,480))
xpos = 50
clock = pygame.time.Clock()
while 1:
    clock.tick(60)
    for event in pygame.event.get():
        if event.type == QUIT:
            sys.exit()
    pressed_keys = pygame.key.get_pressed()
    if pressed_keys[K_RIGHT]:
        xpos += 1
    if pressed_keys[K_LEFT]:
        xpos -= 1
    screen.fill((255,255,255))
    pygame.draw.circle(screen,(0,255,0),(xpos,200),20)
    pygame.display.update()
```

IS THAT WHERE WE ARE? SOME
PLACE CALLED FIRST PROGRAM?

I LIKE IT. IT'S CONCISE
AND MEANINGFUL.

OH BOY.

23

```
pygame.display.set_caption("First Program")
```

This line simply puts a title into the game window. You can write whatever you like but it has to be in quotes. Run the program and check out the top margin of the game window.

```
clock = pygame.time.Clock()
```
and
```
clock.tick(60)
```

The **game loop** loops around many times a second, going just as fast as it can. This means that every time you add in a line of code the whole program slows down a tiny bit, which can change how fast things happen on the screen. To keep things the same on every loop we can put in a clock function. This keeps the loop the same every time.

The "60" in the **clock.tick()** function fixes the time the while loop takes to one sixtieth of a second. A "10" would fix the time taken to one tenth of a second. 60 is just fine for everything we'll be doing just now.

When you add these lines in you'll notice the circle moves a lot slower. This is because the game loop was looping way faster than once every sixtieth of a second before. We can speed up the circle by increasing the amount it moves on each loop. **xpos +=5** might be better.

DID TIME SUDDENLY
SLOW DOWN? HOW COULD

WE TELL?

MEASURE IT WITH A
STOPWATCH.

JUST A SEC. THAT'S NOT
GOING TO WORK.

See if you can make the circle move up and down. You'll have to add in a variable called "**ypos**". Remember you can choose your own variable names. The up and down arrows are "**K_UP**" and "**K_DOWN**".

You'll notice that when you add 5 to **ypos** the circle moves down. On the y-axis positive is down.

It's always important to try stuff out. When you learn a new trick mess around with it. If you want to use a different key on the keyboard most use the "**K_a**" format. So Z would be "**K_z**".

You're probably using the command line a lot now to run your programs. Did you know that pressing the up arrow repeats the last line you wrote? This can be very useful.

I THINK YOU LACK DIRECTION.

WHEN YOU HAVE NO DIRECTION
LIFE'S MORE OF A SURPRISE.

Chapter three

The rain factory...

```
import pygame, sys
from pygame.locals import *
pygame.init()
pygame.display.set_caption("rain")
screen = pygame.display.set_mode((1000,600))
clock = pygame.time.Clock()
rain_y = 0
rain_x = 400

while 1:
    clock.tick(60)
    for event in pygame.event.get():
        if event.type == pygame.QUIT:
            sys.exit()
    screen.fill((255,255,255))
    rain_y +=4
    pygame.draw.line(screen,(0,0,0),(rain_x,rain_y),(rain_x,rain_y+5),1)

    pygame.display.update()
```

We've written a program much like our first moving circle program from page 17.
The rain is going to fall down so we going to change the y position using a variable.
We've called our variable **rain_y**. It changes by 4 with each game loop.

The actual raindrop is a short line.

```
pygame.draw.line(screen,(0,0,0),(rain_x,rain_y),(rain_x,rain_y+5),1)
```

As you might guess we have a line drawing function here. The function works much like the circle and rectangle functions we've already seen. It has five arguments. The first two you are familiar with. The line is drawn on the screen and is black in rgb code. (Feel free to choose different colors.)

The next two arguments mark the beginning and the end of the line. They are coordinates. The first coordinate is the values assigned to **rain_x** and **rain_y**. While the rain drop is falling **rain_y** changes while **rain_x** remains constant.

The other end of the line is given by the second set of coordinates. The **x** value will remain **rain_x** but we add 5 pixels to **rain_y**. This will draw a vertical line 5 pixels long.

The final argument gives us the width of the line, 1 in this case but you could go bigger.

I LOST MY PHONE NUMBER. CAN I HAVE YOURS?

THAT'S MY BEST LINE.

WHAT'S THAT?

IT'S KIND OF FUNNY. BUT IT'S A STARTING LINE, NOT A WINNING LINE.

You'll notice that **rain_x** doesn't change. Rather than create a **rain_x** variable we could have just used the number 400. But lets start the raindrop from a random point at the top of the screen. So rather the write rain_x = **400** we're going to write:

```
rain_x = random.randint(0,800)
```

The **randint()** function grabs a random number from between the two arguments in the brackets. (The numbers in the brackets are inclusive so in this case 0 and 800 could be chosen.)

randint() is stored in Python's **random** module. But we haven't loaded Python's **random** module so at the moment this line won't work. We need to add **random** to the list of modules in the first line of the program. Like this:

```
import pygame, sys, random
```

IT'S RAINING!

I THINK I'M UNDERWHELMED.

Classes

We could create many raindrops by adding in many variables, like rain_x1, rain_x2, rain_x3 etc. And then create many raindrops using those many variables in many pygame.draw.line() functions, one after the other. This would work but it would take a long time and be very boring. As you might guess, we don't do it this way.

What we do is build a factory. In programming this is called a **class**. We use classes to create many copies of the same thing. Each copy is called an **instance** of the class. **Instances** don't have to be identical, and we'll quickly be using classes to create **instances** that are different. Even in our Raindrop class the individual raindrops won't be identical -they will fall in different places.

Over the next few chapters we're going to be learning a lot. We have classes, lists, creating functions and some other important stuff. Unfortunately *all* of this needs doing before we can see the effects of *any* of it. So here's what we suggest. Take a deep, calming breath, lock your little brother out of the room, tell your mum you're doing your homework, and copy the code from page 31 into a new file in whichever text editor you are using.

The program follows a basic structure:

Set up	(Pygame is initialised, modules are loaded, some variables are created.)
Classes	(the instructions for controlling various objects.)
Lists	(where we keep track of all our objects.)
Game loop	(where the action is.)

When writing out the code you'll get some idea of what's going on. When you run the code you will get some falling rain. Over the next two chapters we will explain the code in detail. It can be a little confusing at first but stick with it, read it through a few times if necessary, and all will become clear.

```
import pygame, sys, time, random
from pygame.locals import *
pygame.init()
pygame.display.set_caption("rain")
screen = pygame.display.set_mode((1000,600))
clock = pygame.time.Clock()
raindrop_spawn_time=0

class Raindrop:
    def __init__(self):
        self.x = random.randint(0,1000)
        self.y = -5

    def move(self):
        self.y += 7

    def draw(self):
        pygame.draw.line(screen,(0,0,0),(self.x,self.y),(self.x,self.y+5),1)

raindrops = []

while 1:
    clock.tick(60)
    for event in pygame.event.get():
        if event.type == QUIT:
            sys.exit()

    raindrops.append(Raindrop())

    screen.fill((255,255,255))

    for raindrop in raindrops:
        raindrop.move()
        raindrop.draw()

    pygame.display.update()
```

A closer look at the Raindrop class

```
class Raindrop:
    def __init__(self):
        self.x = random.randint(0,1000)
        self.y = -8

    def move(self):
        self.y += 7

    def draw(self):
        pygame.draw.line(screen,(0,0,0),(self.x,self.y),(self.x,self.y+8),1)
```

IF RAINDROPS HAVE A CLASS DOES THAT MEAN WE DO?

AND IF WE DO, WHO WROTE IT?

First we can see the class is all one big chunk of code. That is, all the lines under the first line are indented.

To create a class we just write the word "class" followed by the name of the class and a colon. It is normal for a class name to start with a capital letter. Remember, this is the name of the blueprint. The things we build from the blueprint, the actual raindrops, will be spelt with a lowercase first letter.

So a **raindrop** is an instance of the class **Raindrop.**

Note that the **__init__** is spelt with two underlines, followed by **init**, followed by two more underlines.

The class is really just a list of functions that control everything to do with a raindrop. Over the next few pages we will have a closer look at the different functions and see what that word **self** does.

But first some general information about functions…

Creating a function

Earlier we said that a function is just something that does something. Python and Pygame already have thousands of functions ready to use. But one of the great things about functions is, like cakes, you can make your own. And it's much easier than making cakes.

Here's how:

Open a new file in your text editor.
Type the following lines:

```
def add(a,b):
    return a+b
```

We create a function using def.

The name of the function is add.

The arguments taken are a and b. (We decide how many arguments are to be taken and what they are called.)

When the function is called it returns the answer to a+b.

Give the file a name (remember not to use spaces; in fact you can only use letters, numbers and underscores) and save it as a .py file.

Open a command line and load Python in the normal way (by typing in Python and hitting return.) When you get the three little arrows type:

import filename

You don't need the .py . In fact, you can't use the .py .

To call the function, type:

filename.add(6,9)

Hit return and you'll get the answer. You've just created a function that adds two arguments.

One we made earlier

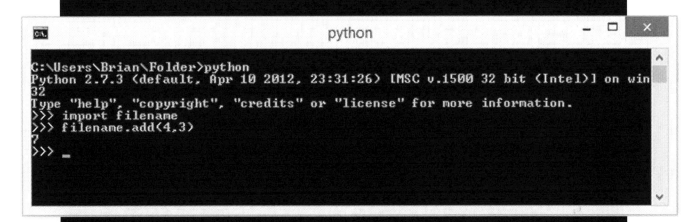

```
python                                    —  ☐  ✕

C:\Users\Brian\Folder>python
Python 2.7.3 (default, Apr 10 2012, 23:31:26) [MSC v.1500 32 bit (Intel)] on win
32
Type "help", "copyright", "credits" or "license" for more  information.
>>> import filename
>>> filename.add(4,3)
7
>>> _
```

You can see we have given the function the two arguments it requires. It has then, using its huge brain, returned the answer.

Of course, we could have called the function whatever we wanted. We could have called it bananas. We could have called it subtract. But it would have still added the two arguments together because that's what we told it to do.

If you put in three arguments it won't work. Try it.

If you put in two words it will work. Python doesn't object to adding words. (There's more about this on page 105.) Try creating some more functions. Go on. It's fun.

If you edit the function in your text editor you will have to save changes and then reload Python in the command line before it will work. To reload Python type quit() at the three little arrows, then return, and then reload Python in the normal way.

```
def __init__(self):
```

Generally you can call your functions what you like but this first function you have to call **__init__()**. The **def** is short for define. What we are doing here is defining our **__init__()** function. **init** is short for initiate. When we create a new raindrop Python will look for the **__init__()** function for the Raindrop class and do what that function tells it to do.

Self

When a new raindrop is created Python gives it a name. We never see or use the name ourselves; it's just for Python to use. But let's imagine the first raindrop created is called raindropone. Python knows raindropone is of the Raindrop class so it fetches the Raindrop class, and everywhere it sees the word "self" it replaces it with the name, raindropone.

When a second raindrop is created it will get a different name. Let's pretend it's called raindroptwo. After Python has used the class to do all it's raindropone stuff it will then replace all the selfs with raindroptwo and do all the raindroptwo stuff.

We only have to write one class but Python can use it many times for all the different raindrops. That is: all the different instances.

OH, AND WHAT ABOUT A FUNCTION FOR
UNCONTROLLABLE LUST. AND LAZINESS. AND ACNE. COOL. AND LET'S NOT GIVE THEM
TELEPATHY AND SPEED OF LIGHT TRAVEL
LIKE ALL THE OTHER UNIVERSES GOT.

GOOD ONE. AND LET'S MAKE THEIR IQ A 100.

A 100? BUT IT WOULD TAKE THEM
THOUSANDS OF YEARS JUST TO FIGURE
OUT WHAT DARK MATTER IS.

IT WOULD TAKE THEM THOUSANDS OF YEARS
JUST TO START WEARING CLOTHES.

YOU'RE SO WICKED. HOW ABOUT
WE GIVE THEM JUST TWO LEGS?

STOP IT, STOP IT. THIS
IS TOO MUCH.

Let's look at the rest of the __init__() function.

```
def __init__(self):
    self.x = random.randint(0,1000)
    self.y = -5
```

Let's imagine a new raindrop has just been created. Python gives the raindrop a name; let's call it raindropfour. The __init__ function replaces the "self" with the name "raindropfour" and gives the raindrop an x and a y coordinate. Raindropfour.x is going to be a random number from 0 to 1000. Raindropfour.y will be -5. We're giving in the value -5 because that places it just above the top of the screen.

Every time a raindrop is created this process will happen. Raindropfive will get an x and a y position, and so on.

Note: **self.x** and **self.y** are variables that have just been created. Where before we created our variables (like xpos and ypos) in that first section of the program, now we are creating them inside a class. Most of the time the variables used by a class are created inside the class.

DO YOU THINK THERE'S A VENDING
MACHINE AROUND HERE?

DON'T DISTURB ME; I HAVE TO
GET THIS DONE LIKE NOW.

The class has two other functions, each created using **def**.

```
def move(self):
    self.y += 7
```

As you can probably figure out, here we have created a function that tells a raindrop how to move. The function is named **move()** and when it is called from the game loop (you'll see that happening later on) it will change **self.y**, that is the y position of a particular raindrop, by 7. That's pretty simple -it makes the raindrop move down the screen. Remember, y is positive going down.

Note: To **call** a function is to make it do its thing.

```
def draw(self):
    pygame.draw.line(screen,(0,0,0),(self.x,self.y),(self.x,self.y+5),1)
```

Here we have created a **draw()** function. When it is called it uses the **draw.line()** function that we first used on page 28 to draw a line. Now we can see how **self.x** and **self.y** are going to be used give the coordinates of the beginning and end of the line.

We can also see how the **draw.line()** function can now draw many different lines. Before we could only use it to draw one line. But now **self** can be used over and over again for raindropone, then raindroptwo, then raindropthree and so on. One line of code can now be used many times. This is the power of classes.

I FOUND PIZZA. WITH PEPPERONI AND CAFFEINE CHUNKS.

I CAN FINISH THIS LATER.

Lists

```
raindrops = []
```

In our program we place this line after the classes, but before the game loop. This line isn't indented.

Remember we have all those raindrops? raindropone, raindroptwo etc. Well, we need to keep track of them. To do this we create a list that's going to hold all the **instances** of the class. We call the list, **raindrops**. It's normal to give lists a small first letter and pluralize the name of the class. The contents of the list are everything between those square brackets. Which is nothing just now. It is possible for us to directly add things to the list; we'll see this in chapter 11. For now, it is only going to be Python that adds things to the list. That'll be raindropone, raindroptwo etc. We will never see these items but Python will keep track of them.

Lists are pretty straight forward but very useful. On the next page you'll see how we persuade Python to add objects to a list.

You should know that lists start at zero. Really our first raindrop would be raindropzero to Python. A list of four items has item numbers: 0, 1, 2 and 3.

WHERE DID SHE GO?

I DON'T KNOW. I HAVE AN 8 CORE 4.7 GHZ PROCESSOR. MORE RAM THAN THE WHOLE OF FRANCE HAD TEN YEARS AGO. I CAN DO THE WHOLE OF HER HIGH SCHOOL MATHS IN THE TIME IT TAKES FOR HER TO SMILE. BUT SHE WANT'S TO GO AND CHEW ON A PIECE OF COOKED DOUGH WITH SOME CHEESE ON TOP.

Creating new raindrops

```
raindrops.append(Raindrop())
```

Append means add to. What we're doing here is adding an instance of the Raindrop class to the list raindrops. Putting this line into the game loop means that in every game loop one raindrop will be added to the list. If we wanted to add two drops per loop, doubling our amount of rain, we could just repeat this line. Like so:

```
raindrops.append(Raindrop())
raindrops.append(Raindrop())
```

You could put in five lines like this. But there is a better way which we show you on page 61 when we've done more on different types of loop.

At the moment the speed the program is running at is limited by that clock tick. We've set it to 60. That is, sixty loops per second. If we turned off that line then the program would go faster and we'd see more rain.

You can turn off a line by placing a hashtag at the beginning of the line.

```
#   clock.tick(60)
```

Your text editor will probably turn the line green. And Python will ignore the line. Sometimes, rather than deleting a line, it's better just to turn it off. This can be useful when experimenting or troubleshooting. Later on we might want to turn the line back on by removing the hashtag. Turning off the clock is fine but it's probably better to keep the clock and add more raindrops per loop.

Keeping track of the raindrops

```
for raindrop in raindrops:
    raindrop.move()
    raindrop.draw()
```

These lines get placed in the game loop underneath the screen.fill() line. They have to go after the screen.fill() line because the raindrops get drawn on top of the filled in screen.

First checkout the info about for loops on page 43.

We are saying that for each **raindrop** in the list **raindrops** Python should apply the **move()** function and the **draw()** function from the **Raindrop class**.

How it works:

The for loop creates the variable called **raindrop**. It then says that **raindrop** is equal to the first item in the **raindrops** list. That is, it turns **raindrop** into **raindropzero**. It then runs the **move()** and **draw()** functions on **raindropzero** before looping back to the beginning. Then it grabs the next item from the list, **raindropone**, and makes that equal to **raindrop**. It then runs the functions on that. It keeps looping back until it has run both functions on all the items in the list. On all the raindrops, that is. And we have hundreds of raindrops.

Pepperoni

So far, we have three different spellings for the word raindrop.

We have **Raindrop** -that name of the class.

We have **raindrops** -the name of the list.

And we have **raindrop** as seen in the **for loop**. This **raindrop** seems to have turned up from nowhere. Well, actually that's true. **raindrop** is a variable that is only used in the **for loop**. We could have used any name. If the **for loop** was written:

```
for pepperoni in raindrops:
    pepperoni.move()
    pepperoni.draw()
```

it would work just as well. Here the **for loop** creates a variable called **pepperoni**. It makes it equal to the first item from the list **raindrops**, which it knows is from the **Raindrop class**. It runs the two functions from the **Raindrop class** and then loops back for the next item in the list. **pepperoni** would be used in the **for loop** but never anywhere else.

MY TUMMY HURTS. WHERE DID THE
PEPPERONI COME FROM? I DON'T KNOW. BUT I THINK THE

VENDING MACHINE WAS RUNNING
WINDOWS VISTA

for loops

A for loop is a little program loop that runs inside the main game loop. It always has the structure: for something in something.

It's generally used to repeat a piece of code for each item in a list of items.

For example:

```
for i in range(5,10):
    print(i * 10)
```

Type this into a new page in your text editor, save the file and then run the file from a command line.

The range() function creates of list of integers from 5 to 9. The for loop then runs the second line for each integer in the list. So our screen will look something like:

```
C:\Windows\system32\cmd.exe          ⚊ ☐ ✗
C:\Users\Brian>python filename.py
50
60
70
80
90
```

Destroying old raindrops

Our **for loop** works nicely. It allows a group of functions to be performed on the items in a list. But we have a problem. We create our raindrops, they fall out of the sky, but they never get destroyed. This means the list gets longer and longer, and uses more and more memory. Even after the raindrops have long since dropped off the bottom of the screen, they are still being controlled from the **for loop**, having their coordinates updated. If we let this happen long enough the list will get so long that the computer won't be able to cope. Python will judder to a halt.

Unfortunately you can't delete items out of a list in a **for loop**. This is because the for loop is going through the list item by item and if it deletes an item it loses track of where it is.

To solve this problem we need to change our **for loop** to a **while loop**, which does allow for items to be deleted from a list. But before we do that we need to create a new function in our **Raindrop** class.

```
def off_screen(self):
    return self.y > 800
```

Here is our new function. We've written it into the raindrop class after the move() function. See the code in the appendix at the back of the book if you're not sure exactly where. The __init__() goes first but after that it doesn't matter what order the functions go in. We always put draw() last but there's no rule.

The second line returns a boolean value. It is saying that if self.y is greater than 800 then **off_screen()** is **True**. Otherwise **off_screen()** is **False**. We will see how this is useful on page 48.

44

Boolean Algebra

Boolean algebra is used everywhere in programming. In Boolean algebra things can only ever be True or False (sometimes we say 1 or 0).

Take an if statement like:

```
if x == 8:
    y +=5
```

Remember:
== means "is equal to"

The first line is looking for a boolean value. If it gets the answer True then is adds 5 to y. If it gets the answer False then it doesn't bother.

In a line like this from page 263:

```
if event.type == KEYDOWN and event.key == K_q and menu == "game":
```

The line is asking if three separate things are true. It will only run the next line if all the statements are true. This is like an *and gate* in electronics.

In a line like this from page 264:

```
if self.x < 0 or self.x > 1000:
```

This line is asking if the first or the second statement is true. If either returns a true then the next line will be run.

We also often use a "not" which can be used to reverse the value of a True or Flase. So the line:

If not A == 30

will return a True if A isn't 30.

If you don't know about Boolean algebra then you should read up on the basics. Try here: computer.howstuffworks.com/boolean.htm

While loops

The **while loop** looks a little more complicated than the **for loop** but it's still pretty easy to use once you get the hang of it. The advantage it has is that we can use it to delete items out of the list once they are no longer needed.

So get rid of the **for loop** and replace it with the following code.

```
i = 0
while i < len(raindrops):
    raindrops[i].move()
    raindrops[i].draw()
    i += 1
```

Now we will talk through each line in the normal way.

```
i = 0
```

Here we are creating a variable called "**i**" and giving it the value zero. As you will see we are going to use it to number the items in the raindrops list.

As always, we don't have to use **i**-we could use anything we wanted as long as it wasn't already being used elsewhere. **avocado = 0** would be fine. But this looping process is called **iteration** so we traditionally use **i**. If **i** is already in use we move on to **j** and then **k**.

```
while i < len(raindrops):
```

This is the beginning of the **while loop**. The **len()** function returns the length of a list. In this case our list called **raindrops**. We are saying that while **i**, which we have just said is 0, is less than the length of the list **raindrops** then the **while loop** will return a **True** and run. If there is nothing in the list then the statement above will not return a **True** and the game loop will just skip to the next block of code.

```
raindrops[i].move()
raindrops[i].draw()
```

These two lines run the two functions from the **Raindrop class**. They are similar to the lines in the **for loop** that run the functions but there are some differences. In the for loop we created a variable called **raindrop** and made it equal to each raindrop in the list in turn. Here we take item number **i** from the **raindrops** list. That's what `raindrops[i]` means -item number **i** from the list **raindrops**.

When the loop first runs, **i** is equal to **0**. There will be at least one item on the list, otherwise the loop can't be running, and the first item in the list will be item number **0**. (Remember list numbers always start at zero.) So here we are running the **move()** and **draw()** functions on the first item on the list.

```
i += 1
```

Then we add one to **i**. The while loop loops back to the beginning and now **i** equals 1. It checks if there is another item on the list by checking if **i** is less than the number of items on the list and then goes again. This time it will be moving and drawing the second item on the list, ie; **raindrop[1]**.

Imagine there were six items on the list. They would be numbered 0,1,2,3,4 and 5. **i** starts at 0 and goes through the items up to number 5. On the next loop **i** would equal 6. The first line of the while loop,

```
while i < len(raindrops):
```

would return a **False,** the **while loop** would stop, and the **game loop** would move on to the next section of code.

When we add an item to the list, using the **raindrops.append(Raindrop())** line, the length of the list goes up by one and the new item goes to the end of the list, where it will be dealt with by the **while loop**.

So far we are just adding raindrops to the list and then looping through the list, moving and drawing each raindrop in turn. But remember, we made that **off_screen()** function to delete raindrops that had dropped off the screen. Now, highlighted, is the magic bit where old raindrops are deleted.

```
i=0
while i < len(raindrops):
    raindrops[i].move()
    raindrops[i].draw()
    if raindrops[i].off_screen():
        del raindrops[i]
        i-=1
    i+=1
```

Beginning with the first highlighted line, we have an **if statement** so we are looking for a **True** or a **False**. We're going to get that answer from the **off_screen()** function in the **Raindrop** class. Remember Python knows to go to the **Raindrop** class because the items in the **raindrops** list were created using the **Raindrop** class.

If you go back and look at the **off_screen()** function you'll see that it detects if a raindrop has gone off the bottom of the screen. If a **True** is returned then the raindrop we're dealing with, raindrop number **i**, gets deleted using the keyword **del**. See page 81 for keywords. We then reduce **i** by one because we've reduced the length of the list by one. Think about this. If we delete an item, let's say we delete item 4 from a list of 8 items, then the next item, item number 5 will become the new item number 4. On the next loop we will want to deal with the new item number 4. Therefore, we have to knock **i** back to 3. The next line in the code adds 1 to **i**, turning it back to a 4. The loop will then move and draw and possibly delete the new item number 4.

48

More randomising

We can make the rain look a little more realistic by randomising the speed at which the rain drops fall. At the moment all the they're all falling at the same rate.

```python
def __init__(self):
    self.x = random.randint(0,1000)
    self.y = 0
    self.speed = random.randint(5,18)

def move(self):
    self.y += self.speed
```

We're going to use the **randint()** function to randomise the speed. We create a variable called **self.speed** and set it to a random number from 5 to 18. (**randint()**'s arguments are inclusive.) We do this in the __init__() function because it only happens once, when a particular raindrop is created. A raindrop then keeps its speed for the whole of its life. If we put the **self.speed** line in the move() function then **self.speed** would change every time the raindrop moved.

When the move() function is called, which is once per game loop for each raindrop, the value of self.speed is added to self.y.

ARE YOU REALLY RANDOM?

I JUST LOOK AT THE WEATHER IN SCOTLAND AND PICK A NUMBER ACCORDINGLY. YOU CAN'T GET MUCH MORE RANDOM THAN THE WEATHER IN SCOTLAND.

Chapter four

Where we get arty...

Images

Let's place an image of Mike on the screen and give him an umbrella to keep off the rain.

If we're going to use images we have to either create them or download them. We drew our character and scanned the image. If you want to use our image you can download it from the website. It's called **Mike_umbrella.png**.

We've used a PNG image. For simple images like this, or for many of the images we use later on made from blocks of color, PNGs works well. For photographic images use JPEGs.

We've made our image 200 pixels high and 170 pixels wide. (In fact we made it much bigger than that then shrunk it down.) Yours doesn't have to be the same size as ours but you should make it roughly the same.

Our image is actually a rectangle with a white background. If you put it on a black page it would look like this:

Pygame, and pretty much everything else, likes its images to be rectangles. Because the color in the **screen.fill()** function is white, the white background on our Mike image won't be noticed. Against a black background, however, we would see that white rectangle. Later on we'll show you a trick to get rid of the white surround.

The pictures printed in this book are in much finer detail than those on the actual game because of the limits of pixel size.

A filing cabinet

You're probably storing your game file in a directory (often called a folder) somewhere. Or maybe it's just on your desktop (which is a directory). If you haven't created a specific directory for your games then you probably should. We created one called: My Games.

In that directory create a new directory. We've called ours: Images. Place your **mike_umbrella** image into your **images** directory. All the images we will use in the games we're going to build will be stored in this directory. You could, of course, create a new directory for each new game you make, and in those directories you'll have an images directory. This would be sensible.

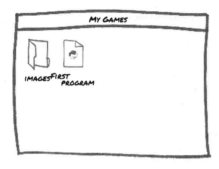

I PRINTED OUT THIS PHOTO OF THE TWO OF US.

COOL. I'LL STICK IT ON MY LAPTOP WITH ALL THE OTHERS.

A Mike Class

First of all we need to load that image of Mike. We do this in the set up part of the program, the place where we created screen and clock. Here we add the line:

```
mike_umbrella_image = pygame.image.load("images/Mike_umbrella.png").convert()
```

In this line we create an object called **mike_image_umbrella**. It's a long name but it makes it clear what we have. Technically **mike_image_umbrella** is a variable but for us creating our first game we can think of it as just the name the program gives the image.

The `pygame.image.load()` function loads the image into Pygame. The `convert()` function is more of a technical thing. It converts the image to a format that your video card can read. It happens automatically anyway every time an image is loaded but by doing it here we save Python the time and effort of doing it every time the image is used.

We created a Raindrop class because we have hundreds of raindrops and a class allows us to create and control all those raindrops with minimal code. There's only going to be one Mike but it still makes sense to create a Mike class. We can then keep all the Mike stuff in one place; everything is neat on the screen.

```
class Mike:
    def __init__(self):
        self.x = 300
        self.y = 400

    def draw(self):
        screen.blit(mike_umbrella_image,(self.x,self.y))
```

So far our Mike class is very simple. As always, we have an __init__() function. Here we have defined self.x and self.y.

We then have a **draw()** function which uses the **screen.blit()** function. To **blit** is to transfer an image from one place to another. Here we take **mike_image_umbrella**, which is an image, and transfer it to the screen. We didn't need to **blit** the shapes earlier because the shape drawing functions in Pygame do the same thing. But we need to **blit** images. Later on we'll also **blit** text.

screen.blit() takes two arguments. The object to be blitted and the coordinates that the object is to be blitted to. Here, **mike_image_umbrella** is blitted onto the screen at the position **(self.x, self.y)**. That's **(300,400)**.

We've created a Mike class that uses the Mike_image_umbrella but we haven't actually created a instance of Mike yet. For the raindrops we created a list in which to store all our instances. Here we only have one instance so we don't need a list. We use the line:

```
mike = Mike()
```

This line can go right after the raindrops list. It creates a single instance of the **Mike** class called **mike**. (Remember classes are also written with () on the end.)

Mike still won't appear on the screen because we haven't called the draw() function from the game loop. It's the draw() function that does the blitting.

```
mike.draw()
```

Mike is going to be drawn over the screen fill but before the raindrops, so add this line in directly after the screen.fill() line.

Now Mike will appear on the screen. It'll be raining but that rain will be going through his umbrella.

Collision Detection

We're going to add a function to the Mike class:

```
def hit_by(self,raindrop):
    return pygame.Rect(self.x,self.y,170,192).collidepoint((raindrop.x,raindrop.y))
```

The first thing we can see is that the function takes an extra argument other than self. It takes an argument called raindrop. At the moment it doesn't know what a raindrop is but it knows it needs one.

We then use something called **pygame.Rect()**. **pygame.Rect()** is actually a class that stores rectangular coordinates. It doesn't draw a rectangle. We could think of it as creating an invisible rectangle that sits over a particular part of the screen. We then detect if a point touches that invisible rectangle by calling the **collidepoint()** function. **collidepoint()** is a function that's part of the **Rect** class (don't worry if this is unclear).

We place the **Rect**, the invisible rectangle, over the top of our Mike image. That is, it's placed at the same coordinates and has the same size as the Mike image. We're doing all this from the Mike class so we can use self.x and self.y. These are the coordinates that the Mike image is placed at. 170 is the width of the Mike image and 192 is the height of the Mike image. By feeding these numbers to Rect we create an imaginary rectangle exactly over the the Mike image.

collidepoint() takes one argument, which will be a set of coordinates given as a tuple. In this example the coordinates are the x and y values of a particular raindrop. So we're checking to see if a raindrop overlaps with the invisible rectangle.

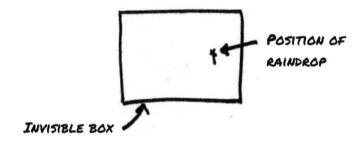

POSITION OF RAINDROP

INVISIBLE BOX

We're going to call the **hit_by()** function from a while loop that's scrolling through the raindrops one by one. (See page 56.) Whichever raindrop the while loop is working on is fed to the **hit_by()** function as an argument. This is the "raindrop" in the first line in the box above.

In summary that second line is returning a True or a False depending on whether a raindrop's x,y coordinate overlaps with the rectangle created by **Rect()**. If we get a True we're going to delete the raindrop from the raindrop list.

```
i=0
while i < len(raindrops):
    raindrops[i].move()
    raindrops[i].draw()
    if raindrops[i].off_screen() or mike.hit_by(raindrops[i]):
        del raindrops[i]
        i-=1
    i+=1
```

We already have a place where we delete raindrops. Now instead of only asking if they're off the screen we're going to ask if they're off the screen **or** hitting Mike. If either one returns a True then bye bye.

Lists and Tuples

We've used lists a fair amount so far. We've seen that creating a list is straight forward.

`raindrops = []` creates a list called raindrops.

We can then easily add things to this list using the append() function, and delete things out of the list using del.

You might remember from earlier on in the book we talked about tuples. Color is always given as a tuple. A tuple is basically a list that you can't change. No appending and deleting. It would make no sense to add another item to the color tuple.

You can create a tuple in exactly the same way you create a list, except you use parenthesis (curved brackets) rather than square brackets. Also tuples have to have at least one comma between the parenthesis (unless it's empty).

A tuple with one item would be: `tupleA=(32,)`

Python would read `tupleA=(32)` as something mathematical rather than a tuple.

In our pong program on page 150 we have a list of bats, and inside that list we have lists of controls. We created the lists using square brackets.

`bats = [Bat([K_a,K_z],10,-1),Bat([K_UP,K_DOWN],630,1)]`

The list of bats and the lists of controls aren't going to change during the game so we could write tuples rather than lists. Tuples have the advantage of being more efficient so you should use them rather than lists if you can. Like this:

`bats = (Bat((K_a,K_z),10,-1), Bat((K_UP,K_DOWN),630,1))`

Don't worry if you don't understand the line. But when you get to page 150 you could come back and look at this.

There's a cloud up in the sky

Let's build a cloud. First we need an image.

Here's our cloud. You can draw your own or download ours from the website. It's called **cloud.png**. First we'll load it into the program. This line goes in the set up at the beginning of the program.

```
cloud_image = pygame.image.load("images/cloud.png").convert()
```

Then we create our very basic cloud class. We'll add some more complicated stuff in later:

```
class Cloud:
    def __init__(self):
        self.x = 300
        self.y = 50

    def draw(self):
        screen.blit(cloud_image,(self.x,self.y))
```

We've set the cloud's x and y coordinates in the __init__() function and then blitted the cloud_image to those coordinates in the draw() function.

```
cloud = Cloud()
```

We then create an instance of the Cloud class in exactly the same way we created an instance of the Mike class on page 54.

```
cloud.draw()
```

Finally we've called the cloud's draw() function. This line can go in the game loop right after right after we call Mike's draw() function.

Very quickly we've built a cloud. Now lets make it a little more cloud like and have the rain falling from just the cloud. At the moment the raindrops are being created in the game loop using the line:

```
raindrops.append(Raindrop())
```

We need to delete this line or turn it off with the hashtag.

When a raindrop is added to the raindrops list the Raindrop class's __init__() function on page 32 (which is called when a raindrop is created) gives the raindrop a random position.

We're going to move both of these actions into the Cloud class. We're going to have a function in the Cloud class that will create a new raindrop and give that raindrop a random position that will then be fed to the Raindrop class.

First, here's what the updated raindrop __init__() function looks like:

```
class Raindrop:
    def __init__(self, x, y):
        self.x =
        self.y =
        self.speed = random.randint(5,18)
```

We can see the __init__() function takes two arguments, x and y, that it didn't back on page 32. These are new values that are going to given to a raindrop when it's created. We'll see this on the following page. We then make self.x equal to x and self.y equal to y. In this way we can give each raindrop coordinates that were created elsewhere.

WHAT ARE YOU DOING?

I'M NOT SURE GRANDMOTHERS ALWAYS TELL THE TRUTH.

I'M TRAINING MY MIND TO CONTROL THE CLOUDS, JUST LIKE MY GRANDMOTHER COULD.

Now we're going to add the following function into the Cloud class we created on page 58. It creates a raindrop and gives it a position.

You might be thinking that we should be creating the raindrop in the Raindrop class but this isn't possible. The Raindrop class can only do stuff when there is a raindrop in existence for it to do stuff to. Instances of a class need to be created outside the class. (There are exceptions to this but that's for another day.)

```
def rain(self):
    raindrops.append(Raindrop(random.randint(self.x,self.x+300),self.y+100))
```

If we simplify the second line above line it looks like this:

```
raindrops.append(Raindrop(x,y))
```

The **Raindrop()** bit is called the Raindrop **constructor**. It creates an instance of the Raindrop class. We've already seen the cloud and mike constructors on pages 54 and 58. So this line adds an instance of the **Raindrop** class to the **raindrops** list.

The instance created is given two values, x and y.

On the previous page we said that when a raindrop is created the Raindrop class's __init__() function demands two arguments, x and y. Well, here they are.

What we actually given it for x is the following:

```
random.randint(self.x,self.x+300)
```

That's a random number between **self.x**, which is the x position of the cloud, and **self.x+300**. The x position of the cloud is its left hand edge. The cloud is 300 pixels wide making the right hand edge of the cloud at **self.x+300**. So the random number is chosen from somewhere between the two edges of the cloud.

For y we give the value **self.y+100**. self.y is the y value of the top of the cloud. The cloud is 108 pixels high. So **self.y+100** is just above the bottom of the cloud.

Now we just need to call the cloud class's rain() function from the game loop. We can do that right from where we call the draw() function.

```
cloud.draw()
cloud.rain()
```

Now let's see about making that cloud move. As with the circle on pages 20 and 22, we need a pressed_keys list.

```
for event in pygame.event.get():
    if event.type == QUIT:
        sys.exit()
pressed_keys = pygame.key.get_pressed()
```

We'll put this after the quit section. It doesn't actually have anything to do with the quit section; this is just where we tend to put this line.

As you might guess, we're going to control the movement of the cloud from inside its class. Let's build a move function:

```
def move(self):
    if pressed_keys[K_RIGHT]:
        self.x+=1
    if pressed_keys[K_LEFT]:
        self.x-=1
```

This looks similar to the code we used to move the circle. We're just changing self.x rather than xpos, and it's inside a function, but it works in exactly the same way.

All we need to do now is call the move() function from the game loop. Well, that's easy. We add in the call with the cloud's other function calls.

```
cloud.draw()
cloud.rain()
cloud.move()
```

Back on page 40 we mentioned a trick for launching more than one raindrop per game loop. We can see in the box above that the rain() function is called once per loop. The rain function launches one rain drop. If we want to launch multiple raindrops we would change the rain() function in the cloud class like this:

```
def rain(self):
    for i in range(10):
        raindrops.append(Raindrop(random.randint(self.x,self.x+300),self.y+100))
```

Here the for loop goes though 10 values of **i**, running the indented line underneath once for each loop. So we get 10 raindrops every time the rain() function is called.

Now we're going to do the simplest of animations. Mike has his umbrella up when it's raining but he doesn't need it when the clouds move away. We're going to load a second image of Mike without his umbrella and make it so he only has his umbrella up when the rain's coming down on him. First we'll load the image.

The image is called Mike.png and is on the website. We load it in the setup part of the program with the line:

```
mike_image = pygame.image.load("images/Mike.png").convert()
```

When it's raining Mike is going to have his umbrella up. But if the cloud moves away so no rain drops are falling on Mike, then the Mike image is going to swap to the one above. In fact, we're going to make it slightly better than that. We're going to make it so it has to have stopped raining on Mike for a whole second before he puts his umbrella down.

To do this we're going to record the time Mike was last hit by a raindrop. Then we can say that if the time since Mike was last hit by a raindrop goes over a second then change to the image above.

We need a clock to tell us the current time (see page 63), and we need to add a variable to store the time Mike was last hit by a raindrop:

```
last_hit_time = 0
```

This variable goes in the set up part of the program.

You might be confused about where we create variables. Is it in a class, in the set up or in the game loop? Generally speaking variables are created in a class if they're used by an instance of that class (like self.x and self.y). They're created in the game loop if they need resetting in every game loop and are only used in the game loop (like **i**). Or in the set up if they're used in the classes and the game loop or just the game loop but get updated rather than reset in each loop. **last_hit_time** will be used in the game loop and a class. It gets updated rather than reset in each loop.

time.time()

Now, it just so happens your computer has a clock in it. This isn't the normal clock which tells you the time in hours and minutes. It's a clock that counts the number of milliseconds since the 1st of January 1970. To see this clock, open up a command line and import Python in the normal way. Then import **time** and run **time.time()**.

```
C:\WINDOWS\system32\cmd.exe - python

Microsoft Windows [Version 6.3.9600]
(c) 2013 Microsoft Corporation. All rights reserved.

C:\WINDOWS\system32>python
Python 2.7.3 (default, Apr 10 2012, 23:31:26) [MSC v.1500 32 bit (Intel)]
32
Type "help", "copyright", "credits" or "license" for more information.
>>> import time
>>> time.time()
1468342556.336
>>>
```

You see that number at the bottom there. That is the number of seconds since midnight on the 1st of January 1970. Python gives us the time in seconds, though many languages give us it in milliseconds.

Midnight on the 1st of January 1970 is called **epoch**.

We are going to take advantage of this clock over the page. But first you should know that if you're going to use this clock you have to import Python's time module on the first line of your program.

```
import pygame, sys, random, time
```

On the 19th January 2038 the number of seconds will get too big for 32 bit unix like computer systems to deal with. This might lead to the death of those systems. It's sometimes called the epochalypse.

WE'RE GOING TO DIE?

NO. BUT SOME OLD COMPUTER SYSTEMS MIGHT.

BUT HOW DO YOU KNOW WE'RE NOT ON AN OLD COMPUTER SYSTEM? EVERYTHING AROUND HERE SEEMS A LITTLE FLAKY. WE DON'T EVEN HAVE COLOR AND THERE'S PEOPLE PLAYING PONG IN A COUPLE OF CHAPTERS TIME.

DAMN. WHERE'S THE ESCAPE POD?

From the while loop we're using to control the raindrops we can see that either of two conditions can trigger the raindrop being deleted. (Lines 5 and 6 below.)

```
i=0
while i < len(raindrops):
    raindrops[i].move()
    raindrops[i].draw()
    if raindrops[i].off_screen() or if mike.hit_by(raindrops[i]):
        del raindrops[i]
        i-=1
    i+=1
```

But now in the second case, Mike hit by a raindrop, we want to delete the raindrop but we also want to record the time that raindrop hit Mike. That is: set **last_hit_time** to **time.time()**. **time.time()** gives us the current time. But we don't want to set last_hit_time if the raindrop has merely gone off the screen. We could try something like this:

```
i=0
while i < len(raindrops):
    raindrops[i].move()
    raindrops[i].draw()
    if raindrops[i].off_screen()
        del raindrops[i]
        i-=1
    if mike.hit_by(raindrops[i]):
        del raindrops[i]
        last_hit_time = time.time()
        i-=1
    i+=1
```

The problem here is that if a raindrop, let's say raindrop number 10 gets deleted in line six then the raindrop looked at by line 8 will be the new raindrop number 10 (the old number 11). This raindrop won't have been moved or drawn or been checked to see if it's off the screen. In the big scheme of things this hardly matters. We're dealing with hundreds of raindrops and if one vanishes for one game loop then so what? But when you're dealing with bullets and the like in the future it might matter.

Another way to deal with this is to replace the second if, on line 8, with an **else**. There's a note on page 65 about if else statements. Basically the else statement is only read if the if statement returns a False.

This would work just fine and you could do it this way. But we're going to show you another way, using flags.

if-else statements

Often in programming we get a bunch of statements that take this form:

```
if x == 3:
    jump up and down
else:
    stand still
```

Here Python reads the first line. If a True is returned then Python makes you jump up and down. Python will then ignore the "else" line. But if the first line returns a False then Python looks at the "else" line and makes you do whatever it says. Python makes you do one or the other but never both.

Multiple if-else statements take this form

```
if x == 5:
    jump up and down
elif x == 6:
    spin around
elif x == 7:
    touch your toes
else:
    stand still
```

As soon as Python finds a True statement it will ignore all the rest. So if x is equal to 6 Python will make you spin around. It will never ask if x is equal to 7. If Python doesn't get a True it will make you do whatever is in the "else" statement

```
i=0
while i < len(raindrops):
    raindrops[i].move()
    raindrops[i].draw()
    flag = False
    if raindrops[i].off_screen():
        flag = True
    if mike.hit_by(raindrops[i]):
        flag = True
        last_hit_time = time.time()
    if flag:
        del raindrops[i]
        i-=1
    i+=1
```

Here we put a flag on each raindrop. So long as the flag stays False then the raindrop doesn't get deleted. But if either condition returns a True then the flag gets set to True. At the end of the loop, when both conditions have returned a True or False, if the the flag is True then the raindrop will get deleted. It doesn't matter if the flag is set to True twice. A True getting set to True is still a True.

Remember the line: `if flag:` is saying: if **flag** returns a True then do the stuff in the lines beneath.

Now any time Mike is hit by a raindrop, **last_hit_time** will update. We can use this in the draw() function on page 67.

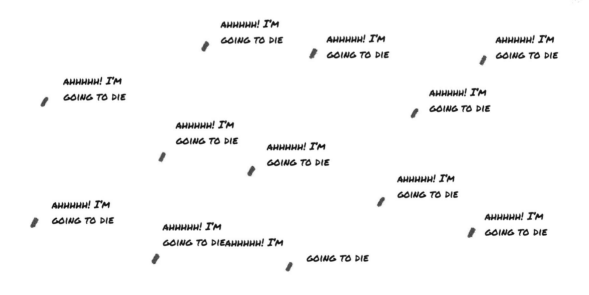

What raindrops are really thinking.

66

```
def draw(self):
    if time.time() > last_hit_time + 1:
        screen.blit(mike,(self.x,self.y))
    else:
        screen.blit(mike_umbrella_image,(self.x,self.y))
```

On page 53 the draw() function was pretty simple. It simply drew the Mike_image at self.x,self.y.

Now we have a condition: `if time.time() > last_hit_time + 1`

Every time a raindrop hits Mike, **last_hit_time** gets updated to **time.time()**. When the draw() function gets called, the difference between **last_time_hit** and **time.time()** will be tiny. **time.time()** won't be greater than **last_time_hit + 1** and we'll get a False. In which case the **else** statement is run and **mike_umbrella** gets blitted.

But if the rain stops hitting Mike then **last_hit_time** will remain the same while **time.time()** continues to count up. After a second **time.time()** will become greater than **last_hit_time + 1**. The if statement will return a True and **mike_no_umbrella** will get blitted. So it takes a second of no rain for Mike fold his umbrella. You can change this number, of course.

THE TIME RULE

WE CAN EITHER GIVE OUR PROJECT ALL THE TIME IT NEEDS. IN WHICH CASE IT WILL NEVER GET FINISHED.

OR WE CAN SET A DEADLINE. IN WHICH CASE WE'LL RUSH TO MEET THE DEADLINE AND THE CODE WILL BE A MESS AND THE PROJECT WILL FAIL.

Chapter five

Where we meet the bad guys...

You know what those clouds
remind me of? Space Invaders.

How are they like Space Invaders?

They move around and they drop
stuff on us. We should blast them
out the sky. That could be kind of fun.

Badguy class

Let's turn that cloud into a bad guy.

- For our bad guys we are going to have to do the usual things. Create a badguy object with an image.
- Create a class so we can have multiple badguys and control them individually.
- Make a list to keep track of the badguys.
- Call badguy functions from the game loop.
- Make them suffer.

On page 71 we have a basic badguy class. Open up a new file in your text editor and type it in. Maybe by the time book three comes out we'll let you cut and paste from the website but for now it's all good practice.

In this program we've created a **Badguy** class, but so far we've only created one bad guy, called **badguy**. **badguy** will appear at a random position at the top of the screen and move down.

Look over the code and try to understand what's going on before reading our explanation. There's very little you haven't seen before.

But first we have to draw our badguy and save the image file into our image folder. We've saved ours as a .png file.

We have made our badguy 70 pixels wide by 45 high and drawn it on a black background.

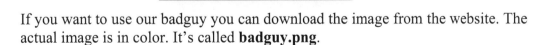

If you want to use our badguy you can download the image from the website. The actual image is in color. It's called **badguy.png**.

```
import pygame, sys, random
from pygame.locals import *
pygame.init()
clock = pygame.time.Clock()
pygame.display.set_caption("Space Invaders")
screen = pygame.display.set_mode((640,650))

badguy_image = pygame.image.load("images/badguy.png").convert()

class Badguy:

    def __init__(self):
        self.x = random.randint(0,570)
        self.y = -45

    def move(self):
        self.y += 3

    def draw(self):
        screen.blit(badguy_image,(self.x,self.y))

badguy = Badguy()

while 1:
    clock.tick(60)
    for event in pygame.event.get():
        if event.type == QUIT:
            sys.exit()

    screen.fill((0,0,0))

    badguy.move()
    badguy.draw()

    pygame.display.update()
```

Here we have a program to create a single badguy moving down the screen. We'll work through this and then start making it a little more exciting.

There's not much in this badguy you haven't already seen. The program is more like the original raindrop from page 31. Here we're blitting an image rather than drawing a line. And we've only created a single instance of the badguy so there's no list and the functions don't need to be called from a for loop or a while loop. At least, not yet.

The badguy gets blitted between 0 and 570 on the x-axis. It's 70 pixels wide so if it's blitted at an x position of 570 then its right hand edge will be touching the right hand edge of the screen.

I THINK THAT'S GOING TO
BE PRETTY EASY TO KILL.

IT'S GOING TO LOSE A RACE
WITH A SNAIL. MAYBE THEY
DON'T HAVE REFINED, WHITE
SUGAR ON THEIR PLANET.

Obviously we can just up the amount we add to self.y each time the move() function is called. That's once every game loop. That would make the badguy zip down the screen but it's not that interesting. We need to make it move around a bit.

Now let's try this for the move function:

```
def move(self):
    self.y += 5
    if self.y > 300:
        self.x +=5
```

Here self.y increases by 5 on every game loop. If self.y is over 300 then self.x also increases by 5

Or how about:

```
def move(self):
    self.y += 5
    if self.y > 150 and self.y < 250:
        self.x +=5
    if self.y > 250:
        self.x -=5
```

I'm sure you can see what's happening here. When the **move()** function gets called the first thing it does is add five pixels to **self.y**. This will make the badguy move down the screen. If **self.y** is greater than 150 but less than 250 then 5 pixels are added to **self.x**. This makes the badguy move to the right as well as down. However, if self.y is greater than 250, we take 5 away from **self.x**. This will make the badguy move to the left.

While we experiment maybe it's worth hashtagging the line that sets self.x to a random number and just setting self.x to 285. Like so:

```
#self.x = random.randint(0,570)
self.x = 285
```

Just so the badguy always goes down the middle of the screen.

MIKE'S BEEN AWAY FOR A LONG TIME; I WONDER
WHAT HE'S DOING. I SAW HIM WITH AN ARC
WELDER AND AN ANGLE GRINDER. MAYBE HE'S
MAKING ME SOMETHING. YEAH, THAT'S PROBABLY
IT. I SHOULD WRITE HIM A POEM OR SOMETHING.

Acceleration

Let's go back to our original move() function:

```
def move(self):
    self.y += 3
```

What we're saying in the move() function is how much **self.y** changes with each loop of the program. In maths, a change in y is called **dy** (and a change in x is called **dx**.) They're pretty much the same as speed. **dx** is speed in the x direction, **dy** is speed in the y direction. If **dy** is zero then you're not moving in the y direction because y isn't changing.

Now let's rewrite the move() function to include **dy**.

```
def move(self):
    dy = 3
    self.y += dy
```

This does exactly the same thing except we have an extra line and an extra variable. It seems pretty pointless.

But suppose we could increase **dy** with each game loop. Suppose we increased it by 1. After two loops self.y would be increasing by 2 pixels. After five loops it would be increasing by 5 pixels. After ten loops self.y would be increasing by 10 pixels. The badguy would be zinging down the screen, getting faster and faster. We would have acceleration.

Acceleration is just speed that increases.

So how are we going to make **dy** change with each loop? Well, we could try something like this:

```
def move(self):
    dy += 1
    self.y += dy
```

Here, each time the **move()** function is called, that is, in every game loop, **dy** increases by 1. That should do it. Unfortunately it won't work. That's because when you create a variable you have to give it a value. Here we try to create a variable, **dy**, but we're not giving it a value, we're just trying to add 1 to its value. So Python gets in a mood and says, what's this **dy**? There is no variable called **dy**. And crashes.

Let's try:

```
def move(self):
    dy = 0
    dy += 1
    self.y += dy
```

Now we have properly created a variable so Python is happy. But every time the move() function is called, **dy** gets reset to zero. Then it's increased by 1, and **self.y** is increased by **dy**, which is, of course, just 1.

We could try is this:

```
def __init__(self):
    self.x = random.randint(0,570)
    self.y = -100
    dy = 0

def move(self):
    dy += 1
    self.y += dy
```

We create the **dy** variable in the __init__() function. The __init__() function only gets called when the badguy is first created so the dy variable won't keep getting reset on every game loop.

But there's a problem here. If you create a variable like this in a function it can only be used in that same function. When the move() function is called, Python will look inside the move() function for a variable called dy. It won't be able to find it because it wasn't created in the move() function, it was created in the __init__() function. It will complain that there was no such thing as **dy**.

We could create the **dy** variable in the set up of the program, up where we define screen and the images. This wouldn't work because each badguy has to have it's own **dy** or they will all end up going at the same speed, and the speed will quickly get very high. Though Python still wouldn't be able to find dy because it would only look inside the move() function.

What we have to do is this:

```
def __init__(self):
    self.x = random.randint(0,570)
    self.y = -100
    self.dy = 0

def move(self):
    self.dy += 1
    self.y += self.dy
```

Adding **self.** onto the front of **dy** means Python will look in the whole class for the variable rather than just inside the function. It also means that when we create multiple badguys a **dy** variable is created for each badguy. It starts with a value (in this case, 0) and gets increased by 1 (in the move() function) with each game loop.

When we write these two functions into the Badguy class we see a badguy that accelerates down the screen.

It goes pretty fast. It might be better with **self.dy +=0.2**

Okay. Now we've shown you how to accelerate objects we're going to leave that for now. We will be using this technique a fair amount in the next book when we introduce more physics into games. Gravity is the obvious example. However, if you want to put accelerating badguys into your game then you should do so.

I GUESS IT FOUND THE CANDY STORE.

THE PRIMITIVE PART OF MY BRAIN THAT WANTS TO SHOOT ANYTHING THAT MOVES JUST SWALLOWED THE LOVE AND PEACE PART WHOLE.

Bouncing off the walls.

Before we start shooting let's make the badguys bounce off the edges of the screen.

```
def __init__(self):
    self.x = random.randint(0,570)
    self.y = -45
    self.dy = 1
    self.dx = 3

def move(self):
    self.x += self.dx
    self.y += self.dy
```

At the moment, if we point our badguys towards the edge of the screen, they fly off the edge. To bounce off the side we are going to create a **self.dx** variable for our badguys in just the same way we created a **self.dy** variable. It's created in the **__init__()** function and given a value. In this case we've given it a value of 3. We can see from the **move()** function that **self.x** will be changing by **self.dx** with every game loop. This means the badguys created will be moving 3 pixels to the right with every game loop from the moment they are created. You can also see they are only moving down the screen by 1 pixel in every game loop. This means they're soon going to fly off the edge of the screen.

THE BADGUYS HAVE GONE OVER TO
THE DARK SIDE.

DOES THAT MEAN THEY'VE BECOME
GOOD GUYS OR BADDER GUYS?

NOT SURE.

We're going to add a couple of lines into the move() function.

```
def move(self):
    if self.x < 0 or self.x > 570:
        self.dx *= -1

    self.x += self.dx
    self.y += self.dy
```

We want the badguys to bounce off the edges. To put that a different way, we want them to reverse their x direction when they touch an edge.

They will touch the left hand edge when **self.x** equals zero. They'll touch the right hand edge when **self.x** equals 570.

The line:

```
if self.x < 0 or self.x > 570:
```

asks if the badguy is touching either of the two sides of our screen. We use < and > rather than == because **self.x** may never actually equal 0 or 570. It's jumping 3 pixels at a time so it might well jump slightly over the edge rather than hit it exactly.

We then point **self.dx** the other way by multiplying it by -1. Simples.

We could take those two lines out of the move() function and create a new function, called **bounce()**, to hold them.

```
def bounce(self):
    if self.x < 0 or self.x > 570:
        self.dx *= -1
```

The reason to do this is really just for neatness. It keeps each chunk of code in a separate place, making it easy to look through the code and see exactly what's going on. You don't have to do this.

Of course, if you do, you have to call the **bounce()** function from the game loop in exactly the same way the move() and draw() functions have been called.

```
badguy.move()
badguy.bounce()
badguy.draw()
```

While we're messing around with functions, let's add in something to detect a badguy moving off the bottom of the screen. This function goes in the Badguy class. We've done pretty much the same with the raindrops on page 44.

```
def off_screen(self):
    return self.y > 640
```

We're going to use this function to create a new badguy when the old badguy goes off the bottom of the screen:

```
if badguy.off_screen():
    badguy = Badguy()
```

We place these lines after the move(), bounce() and draw() function calls on the previous page.

badguy is our bad guy. Here we're telling Python to run the **off_screen()** function on **badguy**. If we get a True then looks at the second line, which contains the Badguy constructor. This line creates a new instance of the Badguy class called **badguy**.

But wait. We already have an instance of the Badguy class called **badguy**. That's the one that just hit the bottom of the screen. When Python creates the new **badguy** it simply dumps the old one in the garbage. So now we'll get a new **badguy** zinging down the screen.

(In the final game we will have a list of badguys. When a badguy goes off screen we'll delete it off the list.)

Adding some randomness

```
def __init__(self):
    self.x = random.randint(0,520)
    self.y = -100
    self.dy = random.randint(2,6)
    self.dx = random.choice((-1,1))*self.dy
```

Here we've set dy to be somewhere from 2 to 6 pixels per game loop. We're giving dx the same magnitude as dy but we want dx to go left or right (positively or negatively) so we're using the **random.choice()** function to multiply the dy value by either 1 or -1.

We could have set dx using the line:

```
self.dx = random.randint(-6,6)
```

This works just fine, but it does mean that self.dx could be one or zero. This would make the **badguy** go straight down or only going slightly left or right. You might want this to happen, so by all means do it this way if you want. We just thought it was worth showing both ways. Quite often in games you want things to move either left or right. The **random.choice()** function is a good way of doing this. In **random.choice()** the random number is selected from the list (technically a tuple) of numbers you place inside the parenthesis. There can be as many numbers as you want. There are two sets of parenthesis, one for the function and one for the tuple.

Note we have placed the self.dx line after the self.dy line because the self.dx line uses self.dy. If these two lines were the other way around we would be trying to use self.dy before we had created it. Python wouldn't like this.

Keywords

Earlier on we talked about using the append() function to add to lists, and del to remove items from lists. append() is a function but del isn't. So what is del?

Python comes with a bunch of keywords, such as while, for, in and del. There are 31 of them at the moment and they do specific tasks. You should know that you aren't allowed to use these keywords as names for variables. Python will moan if you try.

Here is a list of the current keywords:

```
and         elif        if          print
as          else        import      raise
assert      except      in          return
break       exec        is          try
class       finally     lambda      while
continue    for         not         with
def         from        or          yield
del         global      pass
```

You'll notice a few terms that we've used already and we'll be using a few more further on in the book.

Chapter six

There's thousands of 'em...

Creating multiple badguys

We've seen multiple raindrops; we're going to use the same technique for making multiple badguys. We already have a class; now all we need is a list and a while loop to deal with the different instances.

Here's the list:

```
badguys = []
```

As with the raindrops, we create a list to store the badguys. This goes after the class, replacing the line that created the single badguy that read:

badguy = Badguy()

Remember, a lower case first letter and pluralised for lists. Again, this is a convention; you don't have to do it like this but you certainly should.

```
i = 0
while i < len(badguys):
    badguys[i].move()
    badguys[i].bounce()
    badguys[i].draw()
    if badguys[i].off_screen():
        del badguys[i]
        i -= 1
    i += 1
```

Where before we called all the functions one after another in the game loop, we now have to put them inside a while loop.

The **while loop** goes through the list of badguys, calls the **move()**, **bounce()** and **draw()** functions, and detects if the **off_screen()** function returns a **True**, in which case it deletes that badguy off the list. This is pretty much what we did with the raindrops on page 48.

If we run the program you'll notice that nothing happens. You just get a blank screen. This is because we haven't created any badguys yet. Our list is empty. Let's get onto that next.

For the raindrops we just had the line:

```
raindrops.append(Raindrop())
```

This meant a raindrop was created in every game loop. However, creating one badguy per game loop would be far too many. The badguys need to be created just once in a while so we can then have the pleasure of blowing them out the sky. We're going to write some code to launch a badguy every half a second.

First we need to import the time module from Python so we add **time** to the import list at the beginning of our program.

```
import pygame, sys, random, time
```

Next we will create the following variable.

```
last_badguy_spawn_time = 0
```

Okay, it's quite a mouthful. But it does tell us what we're going to use it for, which is to mark the time the last bad guy was spawned. This variable can go in the set up part of the program.

HEY. WHO'S THAT GUY?

```
if time.time() - last_badguy_spawn_time > 0.5:
    badguys.append(Badguy())
    last_badguy_spawn_time = time.time()
```

We place this chunk of code in the game loop right after the quit section. As always, you can check the website or appendix if you're unsure.

Now let's go through what it does.

It asks if the current time (that's **time.time()**) minus the **last_badguy_spawn_time** is greater than 0.5. Well, **last_badguy_spawn_time** is zero so that's going to be true.

Given that it is true it adds an instance of the class **Badguy** to the list **badguys** in much the same way as for raindrops on page 40. It then sets the **last_badguy_spawn_time** to **time.time()**.

When the game loop loops around again **time.time()** will only be slightly greater than **last_badguy_spawn_time**. So **time.time() - last_badguy_spawn_time** will return a false and the next two lines will be ignored. About half a second later the difference between **time.time()** and **last_badguy_spawn_time** will go above 0.5 and a new **badguy** will be created and added to the list.

If we decrease the **0.5** then we will increase the number of badguys appearing.

Cool, huh?

MIKE'S AWAY AGAIN. WHAT
DO YOU THINK HE'S DOING?

WHEN YOU'RE AWAY FROM ME I'M MOSTLY
BATTLING WITH MULTINATIONAL
CORPORATIONS DESPERATELY TRYING TO
PREVENT THEM DOWNLOADING THINGS ONTO
ME THAT I DON'T WANT. I IMAGINE HE'S
DOING SOMETHING SIMILAR.

Now there is one last thing before we put everything together. When you run the program you will notice the badguys have a horrible black rectangle around them that you see when they overlap each other.

This didn't matter when it was just one badguy on a black background but now it's just plain ugly. To fix this we use the following line.

```
badguy_image.set_colorkey((0,0,0))
```

This **set_colorkey()** function sets one color from an image to be transparent. Here we have set black to be transparent. Remember in **rgb** code 0,0,0 is black.

The line can be inserted into the program right after the **badguy_image** line in the set up part of the program.

Now we have a storm of badguys coming out of the sky.

WHAT'S ALL THAT?

THAT'S MY BACKGROUND. ALL THE STUFF ABOUT ME YOU CAN'T NORMALLY SEE.

WHAT'S THAT? IS THIS WHAT YOU'VE BEEN
DOING ALL THIS TIME? DO YOU LIKE IT? IT'S

MY FIGHTER

I FIND YOUR ENTHUSIASM FOR THIS
A LITTLE DISTURBING.

YOU REMEMBER THAT WHEN YOU'RE
BOWING TO THE MARTIAN KING.

Chapter seven

A fighter with teeth...

A fighter class

Let's quickly build a fighter class. First we need an image. You can download ours or build your own. (The picture here is a black and white copy of the color one on the website.) We can add this straight into the badguy program.

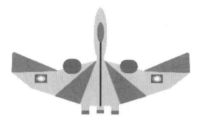

```
fighter_image = pygame.image.load("images/fighter.png").convert()
fighter_image.set_colorkey((255,255,255))
```

The background of the image is white so we're setting the colorkey to white.

Now let's create the class:

```
class Fighter:
    def __init__(self):
        self.x = 320

    def move(self):
        if pressed_keys[K_LEFT] and self.x > 0:
            self.x -=3
        if pressed_keys[K_RIGHT] and self.x < 540:
            self.x +=3

    def draw(self):
        screen.blit(fighter_image,(self.x,591))
```

We're giving it an initial x position of 320. It's y position will never change. It will always be 591 so we're going to write this value straight into the draw() function. We're choosing 591 because the fighter is 59 pixels high and the screen is 650 pixels high so 591 places the fighter exactly at the bottom of the screen.

We've used pressed_keys here so we need to create a pressed keys list right after the quit section:

```
pressed_keys = pygame.key.get_pressed()
```

We have a move() function controlling left and right movement. Looking at the first if statement in the move() function we can see there are two conditions that have to be met before the next line kicks in. The Left key has to be pressed and self.x has to be greater than zero. We have limits to stop the fighter going off the screen. If self.x goes to zero or below, then the second condition returns a False and the fighter won't move any further to the left.

The second if statement works in the same way. The limit is at 540 because the the fighter is a hundred pixels wide so its x-position will be at 540 when the right tip of the wing is touching the right edge of the screen.

We then need to create an instance of the fighter:

```
fighter = Fighter()
```

We've seen a similar lines before. It goes directly after the classes.

And finally we have to call the fighter's draw() and move() functions:

```
fighter.move()
fighter.draw()
```

These two lines need to go into the game loop. The draw() function call has to go after the screen fill otherwise the screen will get filled in over the fighter. Both functions may is well go together so place them right after the screen fill line.

And that's the fighter done. It's getting easy now.

NOW WE NEED SOME RAIN THAT
FALLS UP.

I THINK YOU MEAN HIGH SPEED,
FUTURISTIC PROJECTILES OF
DESTRUCTION.

THAT'S WHAT I SAID.

A missile factory

Missiles are very much like the raindrops. They are launched from something that moves left or right. They move up in a straight line and need deleting once they leave the screen. Let's have a look at a missile class:

```python
class Missile:
    def __init__(self,x):
        self.x = x
        self.y = 591

    def move(self):
        self.y -= 5

    def off_screen(self):
        return self.y < -8

    def draw(self):
        pygame.draw.line(screen,(255,0,0),(self.x,self.y),
↵        (self.x,self.y+8),1)
```

The final line is too long to fit onto a page of this book. In Python, starting a new line means something. (Most computer languages aren't like this.) So we have used the ↵ symbol to show this line is a continuation of the previous line and in the actual code would be all on one line. (There's a note about this on page 108.)

YOU KNOW, I LOVE THE MISSILES. THEY'RE SLICK AND FAST AND THEY SHOOT UP THE SCREEN. THEY'RE RED AND AND FULL OF HIGH EXPLOSIVE AND NOT LIKE RAINDROPS AT ALL. BUT THERE'S A PROBLEM WITH THEM.

I KNOW. THEY NEED A COOL NAME. LIKE A SIDEWINDER OR TOMAHAWK.

You can see that the Missile class is very similar to the Raindrop class. The Missile class's __init__() only takes one argument apart from self. That is **x**, which marks where the missile is launched from. This will change as the fighter moves sideways. The fighter never moves up or down so the initial y position for a missile will always be the same.

The move() function moves the missile up the screen. The off_screen() function returns a True when the missiles moves off the top of the screen.

Now we need to create a missile list:

```
missiles = []
```

We need a list because there are going to be many missiles.

Then we need a while loop from where we can call the missile functions and delete missiles:

```
i = 0
while i < len(missiles):
    missiles[i].move()
    missiles[i].draw()
    if missiles[i].off_screen():
        del missiles[i]
        i -= 1
    i += 1
```

This can go under the similar loop that controls the badguys. You can see that it's pretty much identical.

It doesn't matter that both loops use **i**. **i** gets created then used in one loop, then reset to zero and used in the second loop. One never interferes with the other.

NO. THEY DON'T NEED A
NAME. THEY'RE JUST
MISSILES. NO. THE
PROBLEM IS...I KNOW. YOU WANT THEM TO

BE SELF-GUIDING

Launching a missile

The main difference between the missiles and the raindrops and badguys is how a missile is created. We're going to use a key press to launch the missiles. Like a fire button. This will involve a function in the fighter class that actually creates the missiles and adds them to the missiles list, and some code in the game loop that calls the function when the fire key is pressed.

Place the following function in the fighter class:

```
def fire(self):
    missiles.append(Missile(self.x+50))
```

When a missile is fired from the fighter its initial position is dictated by the position of the fighter. This is why the **fire()** function gets placed in the fighter class. Here we can see that if the **fire()** function is called a missile gets added to the missile list. This is very similar to the rain() function in the cloud class.

Let's just take another look at that second line:

$$\texttt{missiles.append(Missile(self.x+50))}$$

THE CLASS. THIS CORRESPONDS TO THE "SELF" ARGUMENT IN THE MISSILE'S __INIT__() FUNCTION.

THIS IS THE ARGUMENT "X" IN THE MISSILE'S __INIT__() FUNCTION. (WHICH IS THE FIGHTER'S X POSITION (SELF.X) PLUS 50.)

This is a little simpler than the rain() function because we don't have to give a random position for the missile. It's always going to come out of the nose of the fighter which is the fighter's x-position plus 50 pixels. The fighter is 100 pixels wide.

You might be wondering why there is no comma between the arguments. The **Missile()** is the missile **constructor**. The **xpos+50** is an argument in the missile constructor. The missile constructor is itself an argument in the **append()** function. When we create a new object we use a constructor that in turn contains the arguments demanded by the class's __init__() function.

Note: You might think you should put the **fire()** function in the Missile class. After all, it's the missile that gets fired. But remember we can't do that because until a missile gets fired there aren't any missiles in existence to have a function called.

A fire button

```
for event in pygame.event.get():
    if event.type == QUIT:
        sys.exit()
    if event.type == KEYDOWN and event.key == K_SPACE:
        fighter.fire()
pressed_keys = pygame.key.get_pressed()
```

The first thing to notice about this block of code is where it is placed. It is inside the **for loop** that we first explained on page 9 to allow us to quit the game. The event type we were looking for then was a mouse click on the ❎ icon. (That's what the "**QUIT**" means.) The new if statement we have added is looking for a **KEYDOWN event**.

KEYDOWN detects if a key has gone from not being pressed to being pressed. If a key was already pressed then **KEYDOWN** won't detect it. **KEYUP** detects the opposite. The **pygame.key.get_pressed()** function we first saw on page 22 detects if a key is being held down.

The first line: **for event in pygame.event.get():** detects things like key presses and mouse clicks and creates a list of those events.

The first part of our new highlighted if statement (before the **and**) asks if any events in that list were keys going from not being pressed to being pressed. The second part asks if one of those keys was the space key.

It is important we ask if there was a **KEYDOWN** event before we ask if it was the space key being pressed. If we miss the first part then the game will crash, if we miss the second part then any key, not just the space key, will return a True.

If the if statement returns a True then the fighter.fire() function is called and a missile is created.

If we hold the space key down only one missile will be created because the **KEYDOWN** event only happened once.

I'M NOT SURE HOW TO CREATE SELF GUIDING MISSILES BUT BY THE TIME WE GET ONTO THE NEXT BOOK I'LL BE ABLE TO DO THAT.

SELF GUIDING WOULD BE COOL, BUT THAT'S NOT THE PROBLEM.

Using a missile image

Although many games just use a short line for a missile you might want to use an image. You already know how to do this. First, an image.

We've called ours **missile.png** and you can download it from the website if you want. When creating images that are only a few pixels wide it's hard to get in any detail. The black and white image above has far more detail than the image on our website because it's being printed in a book.

In the set up part of the program we add the lines:

```
missile_image = pygame.image.load("images/missile.png").convert()
missile_image.set_colorkey((255,255,255))
```

Then the draw() function in the Missile class becomes:

```
def draw(self):
    screen.blit(missile_image,(self.x,self.y))
```

Of course our missile is wider than just a single pixel. Ours is 8 pixels wide. The code above will place the left hand edge of the missile in the centre of the fighter. So to line it up properly we shift the missile's x coordinate to the left by half the width of the missile.

Like this:

```
def draw(self):
    screen.blit(missile_image,(self.x-4,self.y))
```

DO YOU WANT THEM TO BE FASTER OR BIGGER OR A DIFFERENT COLOR?

NO.

Chapter eight

Killing bad guys...

Collision detection

THEN WHAT'S THE PROBLEM? THEY DON' 'N THE BADGUYS!

We've already done some collision detection between the raindrops and Mike on page 55. There we used the pygame.Rect().collidepoint()function that detects collisions between rectangles and points. Here we're going to detect collisions between circles and points. There is no function that does this for you so we have to do it the hard way, using some maths. (It's not that hard.)

You could treat the badguys as rectangles and use the Rect().collidepoint() function. The function would look like this:

```
def touching(self,missile):
    return pygame.Rect((self.x,self.y),(70,45)).collidepoint(missile.x,missile.y)
```

If you're not sure what's going on check out page 55.

But we're doing circles just to show you something new. Below is the function that treats a badguy as a circle and detects if it's touching a missile. As with the alternative above, this function goes in the Badguy class.

```
def touching(self,missile):
    return (self.x+35-missile.x)**2+(self.y+22-missile.y)**2 < 1225
```

First, notice that the **touching()** function takes the argument **missile.** This argument is provided when the function is called. If you look on page 99 you'll see that the function is called from a **while loop** that is going through a list of missiles. So the argument is just the **missile** that the while loop is dealing with at that moment.

We are treating the badguy as a circle. The function returns true if the distance between the centre of the badguy and the missile is less than 35 pixels. We're using Pythagoras theorem to detect this.

1225 is 35^2. We could equally write 35**2 in the program but we happen to know 35^2 is 1225. As you have no doubt figured out, **2 is Python for squared.

The **touching()** function will return a True or a False.

Some Pythagoras.

Centre of the badguy coordinates:
(self.x+35,self.y+22)

Remember, self.x and self.y
are the coordinates of the
top left of the badguy
image.

Missile coordinates:
(missile.x , missile.y)

Note:
Our badguy image is
70x45 pixels. Yours
might be different.

missile →

We know from Pythagoras that A^2 is equal to $B^2 + C^2$

We can say that the missile is touching the badguy if A is less than the radius of that circle around the badguy. That's 35 pixels. That's the same as saying A^2 has to be less that 1225 (that's 35^2). This is also the same as saying $B^2 + C^2$ must be less than 1225.

B is (self.x + 35) - missile.x

C is (self.y + 22) - missile.y

So if $((self.x + 35)-missile.x)^2 + ((self.y\ 22)-missile.y)^2$ is all less than 1225 then the missile is touching the badguy.

This is why they teach Pythagoras at school. They know that one day you'll have to go to war with a fleet of marauding aliens.

In the game loop, down below the two chunks that move and draw the badguys and missiles, we're going to add the following piece of code.

```
i = 0
while i < len(badguys):
    j = 0
    while j < len(missiles):
        if badguys[i].touching(missiles[j]):
            del badguys[i]
            del missiles[j]
            i -= 1
            break
        j += 1
    i += 1
```

So what's going on here? It looks similar to the while loops from pages 48 and 83. The difference is that we have a second loop going on inside the first loop.

We begin with the first badguy in our list of badguys. The number of the badguy is given by `i`. For that one badguy we then loop through the positions of all the missiles on the screen, checking if any of them are touching the badguy. That's the `j` loop. We then go onto the next `i` and do all the `j`'s again. So we have an `i` loop and inside that loop we have a bunch of `j` loops.

If we discover a missile touching a badguy then we delete both the badguy and the missile and move onto the next badguy. If nothing touches then we loop back to check the next badguy.

That **break statement** (this kind of thing is generally called a statement) stops the loop. We have just deleted the badguy and the missile so we don't want to be trying to detect collisions between items that don't exist anymore. We only break the `j` loop. Then add 1 to `i` and go back to the beginning; after all, another badguy may have been hit elsewhere on the screen. We don't have to minus 1 off the `j` loop here because we're going to start again from the beginning of the `j` loop anyway.

In summary, this chunk of code goes through each badguy and checks if any missile is touching it. If so, it deletes them both. If you still can't quite see what's going on imagine each list is five long and badguy#2 and missile#2 are touching . Go through the loop seeing what happens. Remember the **break** spits you out of the j loop so the next line would be `i += 1`.

If you do this you'll see that on the next `i` loop we'll be dealing with the new badguy#2. But the j loop will start from zero again and we'll deal with all the missiles currently on the list, which will be one less than last time. (Unless a new one has just been fired.)

Chapter nine

Where we find out the score...

Finding the score

```
score = 0
font = pygame.font.Font(None,20)
```

First we add these two lines into the set up of our program. It's kind of obvious what the first line does. It creates a variable called **score**.

The second line creates the font in which the score will be written.

Let's just go through that line. We're finding the Pygame module; in that we're finding the font module; and in that we're finding the Font class. From the Font class we're not actually selecting a font. By writing in "None" we're telling Pygame just to choose the operating system's default font.

The "20" is setting the font's size.

WHEN I SPEAK ALL THAT HAPPENS IS THESE WORDS APPEAR IN THE SKY. I DON'T MIND, BUT I DON'T WANT MY VOICE TO BE IN SOME OPERATING SYSTEM'S DEFAULT FONT. THAT JUST SEEMS LAZY.

DON'T WORRY. YOU SPEAK IN A FONT CALLED PERMANENT MARKER. THE FONT WAS DESIGNED BY A COMPANY CALLED FONT DINER

If we wanted to choose a specific font, like comic sans ms, we would write a line like this:

font = pygame.font.SysFont("comicsansms", 20)

Operating systems come with a bunch of fonts preloaded. To find out which fonts you have available you can use our old favourite, the command line. Load up Python in the usual way. Then at the three little arrows type: **import pygame**

At the next set of arrows type: **pygame.font.get_fonts()**

And hit return. You'll get a list of all the fonts available.

So we've created the score variable and the font in which the score will be written.

Now we are going to create a **score()** function inside the badguy class. We do this in the usual way. We find our badguy class and add in the following lines into our list of functions. It doesn't matter what order the functions go in. We're adding score into the badguy class because score is going to change when a badguy gets deleted. It's easy to think the score should go into the fighter class but really the score is nothing to do with the fighter; it changes when badguys die.

```
def score(self):
    global score
    score+=100
```

Now what does that **global score** mean?

When we want change variable inside a function Python only looks for that variable inside the function or, if it has a **self** stuck on the front, in the class. But sometimes we need to change a variable that was created outside both the function and the class. Score has a purpose outside the class. So we write **global score**. This tells Python that **score** is elsewhere in the program. Python then trundles off to find it. Without that **global** Python would never look outside the function.

If you're thinking we could create score in the __init__() function and use **self.score** here in the **score()** function, then remember that in the __init__() function we are creating a particular badguy. We don't want the score to increase just for that badguy. The score is for the whole game. That is: it's global.

The final line tells Python to add a 100 to **score** every time the **score()** function is called.

We need to call the score() function every time a **missile** hits a **badguy** so let's place the function call in the section of code that detects collisions between missiles and badguys.

Like so:

```
i = 0
while i < len(badguys):
    j = 0
    while j < len(missiles):
        if badguys[i].touching(missiles[j]):
            badguys[i].score()
            del badguys[i]
            del missiles[j]
            i -= 1
            break
        j += 1
    i += 1
```

We have to call the **score()** function before we delete the badguy otherwise we won't have a badguy from which to call the **score()** function.

I'M GLAD WE'VE GOT A SCORE. WHAT'S THE POINT OF SHOOTING ALIENS IF WE DON'T KNOW HOW MANY WE'VE BLASTED?

TOTALLY. WHEN THEY WIN THE WAR THEY NEED TO KNOW YOU KILLED MORE OF THEIR BABIES THAN ME.

Placing text on the screen

Our program knows the score but hasn't written it onto the screen yet. To do this add the following line into the end of the game loop, just before the display update.

```
screen.blit(font.render("Score: "+str(score),True,(255,255,255)),(5,5))
```

We've seen **screen.blit()** before (page 53). And, as before, we're using it to place something on the screen. The **blit()** function is expecting two arguments: the object to be blitted -some text in this case- and the position it's to be blitted at.

The object to be blitted is contained in the **font.render()** function. To render something is to create an image out of something. Here we are rendering the score in the font we created earlier.

font.render() takes three arguments. The first argument is the stuff to be rendered. We are rendering two things. The first is the text inside the quotes. That is: "**Score:** " including the space. After the word Score we want to write in the value of the **score** variable. But the **score** variable is a number. If you try to render a number you'll get a error. So **str(score)** turns the numerical value of **score** into a **string** (see page 105) that can then be rendered and blitted onto the screen. The plus sign just adds the two strings ("**Score:** " is a string) that are to be rendered together, making one long string.

The next argument is that word, **True**. This turns on the **antialiasing**. **Antialiasing** is a method of smoothing out the jagged edges on characters when they are displayed on the screen.

Then we set the color of the text -white in this case. That's the third argument.

Finally, we have the second argument in the **blit()** function (remember font.render() was the first argument in the **blit()** function) giving the position of the text. As with rectangles, the position marks the top left hand corner. So here the top left hand corner of the text will be at the point 5,5 on the screen.

Strings

Like God and your maths teacher, Python doesn't really like it when you try to add a word to a number. It understands a number plus a number. 3+4=7. And it can add a word to a word. Love + able = Loveable. But when you try to add a word to a number Python gets in a huff.

A row of characters, like a word or even just a random bunch of letters, is called a string. Strings always go in quotes and you can add strings together like this:

"qwerty" + "asdf" is "qwertyasdf"

You can do this from the command line. Load Python and try it.

Sometimes we need numbers that are really letters but that look exactly like numbers. This is what the str() does. It turns numbers into strings.

So while 75+75 is 150

str(75) + str(75) is "7575"

When score = 57:   Str(score) + "75" iss 5775. By placing the 75 in quotes we have turned it into a string.

Putting score into quotes Like this: "score" won't get you 57 as a string. It's just turned your variable name into a string so you'll get the word: score.

Str(score) + 75 won't go down so well because you can't add a string to a number.

"Score: " +str(57) is Score: 57 because we're adding two strings.

"Score: " + "57" will also render as Score: 57

You can experiment with this stuff in the command line. Also note that it doesn't matter if you use single quotes or double quotes just so long as you're consistent.

Chapter ten

Game over...

Getting hit

We haven't quite got a complete game yet. We have badguys, missiles, a score and a fighter that we can control. But at the moment we can't lose.

For this game we are going to make it game over when the fighter gets hit by a badguy. As you might guess, we are going to create a function that detects a collision between a badguy and the fighter. This function will go into the fighter class.

```
def hit_by(self,badguy):
    return (
            badguy.y > 546 and
            badguy.x > self.x - 70 and
            badguy.x < self.x + 100
            )
```

We've written this is a slightly strange way and you can read why on the opposite page. There are only two lines of code here; one beginning **def**, and one beginning **return**. In that second line you can see there are three conditions to be met. The line is basically saying:

> Return a True if condition A *and* condition B *and* condition C are all true.

Condition A is that **badguy.y** is greater than 546.

That means the badguy's **y** position has to be over 546. Why 546?

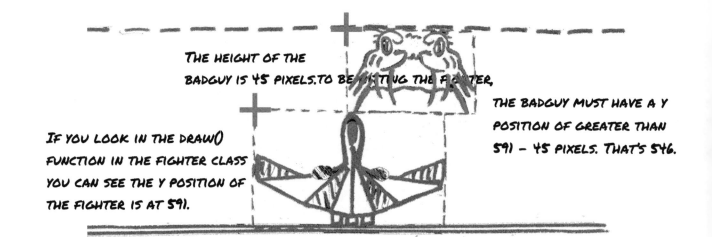

THE HEIGHT OF THE BADGUY IS 45 PIXELS. TO BE HITTING THE FIGHTER,

THE BADGUY MUST HAVE A Y POSITION OF GREATER THAN 591 - 45 PIXELS. THAT'S 546.

IF YOU LOOK IN THE DRAW() FUNCTION IN THE FIGHTER CLASS YOU CAN SEE THE Y POSITION OF THE FIGHTER IS AT 591.

Splitting Lines

If we want to shorten our lines of code so they aren't stretching for miles across our screen, we can break a line after a term inside a pair of brackets. Python knows everything inside brackets should be on one line and reads it as such.

So a draw() function could be written like this:

```
def draw(self):
    pygame.draw.line(screen,(255,0,0),(self.x,self.y),
(self.x,self.y+8),1)
```

In this situation Python ignores the indents so you could write the function like this:

```
def draw(self):
    pygame.draw.line(screen,(255,0,0),(self.x,self.y),
    (self.x,self.y+8),1)
```

Another method is to use a back slash before or after an operator. Make sure there's no space after the back slash

Like this:

```
y =   3+4+\
      5+6
```

Though Python programmers generally add in extra brackets:

```
y = (3+4+
     5+6)
```

Here we've gone even further:

```
Return  (
        condition A and
        condition B and
        condition C
        )
```

Often code is written like this for neatness sake. All this could be on a single line in the code in your text editor but sometimes we would actually write the code like this. It makes the code easy to read.

The next condition that has to be true is:

```
badguy.x > self.x - 70
```

70 PIXELS THE BADGUY'S X-POSTION HAS TO BE GREATER THAN THE FIGHTER'S X-POSITION MINUS 70, OTHERWISE IT CAN'T POSSIBLY BE TOUCHING THE FIGHTER.

And the last condition that must be true is:

```
badguy.x < self.x + 100
```

HERE WE SEE THAT THE BADGUY'S X-POSITION MUST BE LESS THAN THE FIGHTER'S X-POSTION PLUS A 100, OTHERWISE THE BADGUY CAN'T POSSIBLY BE TOUCHING THE FIGHTER.

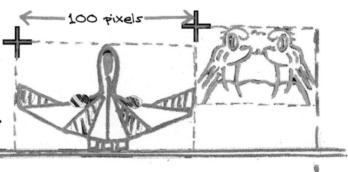

100 pixels

We can see that if all three of these conditions are true then the badguy must be touching the fighter. In this case our **hit_by()** function returns a true.

It could be that these three conditions are true but that the badguy is underneath the fighter. We don't have to worry about this because if the badguy is underneath the fighter, then it's off the bottom of the screen and has been destroyed by the badguy's **off_screen()** function. If we didn't have this **off_screen()** function we would have to add in a forth condition to check the bottom edge of the fighter and the top edge of the badguy were overlapping.

There is a function that does collision detection between two rectangles. It's called: **pygame.Rect.colliderect()**. We'll use this later on. To be honest it doesn't save much time. Doing it this way also gives you more of an idea of what is actually going on.

There is a situation in which the three conditions might be true but the badguy and the fighter aren't actually touching.

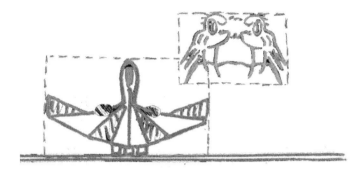

Here the rectangles around the images are overlapping but the images themselves are are not. Python would call this a hit but someone playing the game might not agree.

We have used Pygame's rectangle system to keep things simple. To use the actual shapes of the images and then work out it they are overlapping is too complicated for this book. A quick fix might be to shrink the fighter rectangle to something like this:

So now our function would have slightly different numbers.

```
def hit_by(self,badguy):
    return badguy.y > 585 and badguy.x > self.x - 55 and badguy.x < self.x + 85
```

Of course, it would mean that this wouldn't be a collision. We think that's okay. It's up to you to decide what works best for you.

Another solution is to draw the fighter and invader to be more rectangular.

Dying

Now we have a function that tells us if the fighter and badguy are colliding we have to use it. We're going to put the following chunk of code towards the end of the game loop, right after the line where we screen.blit() the score. Note: We now have two lines reading: **pygame.display.update()**. One in the chunk below and the original one in the game loop. Check the code on the website or at the back of the book if you want to be sure you've placed this chunk correctly.

```
for badguy in badguys:
    if fighter.hit_by(badguy):
        while 1:
            for event in pygame.event.get():
                if event.type == QUIT:
                    sys.exit()
            pygame.display.update()
```

This might look a little strange. What we're doing here is stopping the game. We're going about it in a slightly strange way. When you're working at Nintendo you probably won't use this method, but just here it works and it's easy to do. That counts for a lot.

So what are we doing?

Well, those first two lines look for for any **badguy** in the list **badguys**, and calls the **fighter.hit_by()** function we just created. If the **hit_by()** function returns a False, then the program fetches the next **badguy** off the list and tries again. If we get a False on all the **badguys** then game loop ignores the rest of this chunk and moves on with the game.

But if the **hit_by()** function returns a True then we get into the while loop. **while 1:** simply starts a loop that will keep going. The code inside the while loop we saw back on page 9 and is simply the code that allows you to quit the while loop as well as the display update.

What we're doing here is starting a **while loop** that will loop forever inside our game loop. The game is simply caught, forever running in a little circle that does nothing. On screen it looks as if the game has frozen. The only way out of this while loop is to quit the game using quit button.

So when you get hit by a badguy, the game freezes. Simple as that.

Maybe that's too simple. Let's add in a game over screen and a final score.

Oh, and if the game's too easy, feel free to speed up the badguys or increase their numbers by reducing the delay between each one getting created.

Here's our game over screen:

You can always create your own. Ours is available on the website. It's 300 pixels wide by 244 pixels high.

First of all we need to create a variable to store the image just as we have with all the images so far.

```
GAME_OVER = pygame.image.load("images/gameover.png").convert()
```

This goes at the beginning of the program together with the other image variables.

TO DIE IN BATTLE IS GLORIOUS.

YOU'LL ALWAYS BE REMEMBERED, MIKE. LONG AFTER YOUR BATTLE SCARRED BODY HAS TURNED TO PIXILATED DUST.

The line that's going to blit the GAME_OVER image needs to be triggered when a fighter gets hit but before we get caught in the while loop we just created.

Like so:

```
for badguy in badguys:
    if fighter.hit_by(badguy):
        screen.blit(GAME_OVER,(170,200))
        while 1:
            for event in pygame.event.get():
                if event.type == QUIT:
                    sys.exit()
            pygame.display.update()
```

Here we blit the image we have stored in the GAME_OVER variable at the coordinate: 170, 200.

As you can see from our game over screen, we also need to blit some numbers. We have Total Shots, On Target, Missed, Accuracy and Score.

ARE YOU SURE ABOUT THE GLORIOUS DEATH THING?

I'M HAVING SECOND THOUGHTS.

We already have a variable called **score**. Let's add in Total Shots (which we'll just call **shots**), On Target (which we'll just call **hits**), and **misses**. We don't have to worry about **accuracy** because that will be worked out with some maths using the other variables.

So add:

```
shots = 0
hits = 0
misses = 0
```

These can go under the score variable in the set up part of the program.

Now, let's go through the program and add in lines where these variables need updating. The score has already been done.

First, the shots. This needs to increase by one every time a missile is fired. So we need to add a line to the **fire()** function in the **Fighter class**. Remember **global** from page 116? We have to tell the function that **shots** is global.

```
def fire(self):
    global shots
    shots+=1
    missiles.append(Missile(self.x+50))
```

We've put **shots** in the fire() function but it could have gone in the game loop where the button press that fires the missile is detected. Placed there, we wouldn't need the global line because we wouldn't be inside a function. Either place will do.

87% OF STATISTICS ARE MADE UP.

The next variable is **hits**. A hit is when a missile hits a badguy so we're going to place this in the loop that detects collisions between missiles and badguys.

```
i = 0
while i < len(badguys):
    j = 0
    while j < len(missiles):
        if badguys[i].touching(missiles[j]):
            badguys[i].score()
            hits += 1
            del badguys[i]
            del missiles[j]
            i -= 1
            break
        j += 1
    i += 1
```

You can see we have our **hits +=1** line right under our **badguys[i].score()** line. The two lines do a very similar thing in a different way. **hits** goes up by 1 every time a hit occurs, score goes up by 100.

We could have dealt with hits in the same way we dealt with score. That is, build a function. Or we could have dealt with score in the way we dealt with hits. A third option would be to work out hits at the end by making hits equal to score divided by 100. All these options are valid. As we've said before, it's up to you exactly what you do, just so long as it works.

There is a reason we put score into a function. In the future we might want to add different kinds of badguy. A badguy type2 and type3. Badguy type2 might add a different score. How to use a class to create two similar but not exactly the same objects, like badguys, is something we will cover later on.

So by keeping score and hits separate it gives us more freedom to mess around with score later on.

Next, the misses:

```
while i < len(missiles):
    missiles[i].move()
    missiles[i].draw()
    if missiles[i].off_screen():
        del missiles[i]
        misses += 1
        i -= 1
    i += 1
```

Every time a missile goes off the top of the screen we are going to add 1 to the misses score. Add this in right after the line that deletes a missile. There's no reason to build a function, and no function to which this line could be added.

Remember, the off_screen() function doesn't only run when a missile goes off the screen. It runs once for every missile in every game loop. It's only when the off_screen() function returns a True that we want to add 1 to the misses. This happens in the chunk of code above.

OH. YOU'RE BACK, ARE YOU?

YEAH. I'M A FLESH
EATING ZOMBIE NOW.

COOL.

Now we need to display the numbers associated with those variables over the top of the GAME-OVER image. We place the lines after the screen.blit(GAME_OVER) line but before the while loop that freezes the game.

```
screen.blit(GAME_OVER,(170,200))

screen.blit(font.render(str(shots),True,(255,255,255)),(266,320))
screen.blit(font.render(str(score),True,(255,255,255)),(266,348))
screen.blit(font.render(str(hits),True,(255,255,255)),(400,320))
screen.blit(font.render(str(misses),True,(255,255,255)),(400,337))
screen.blit(font.render(str(100*hits/shots)+"%",True,(255,255,255)),(400,357))

while 1:
```

Here we see how each number is placed on the screen. We've seen this kind of line already with the score on page 104. We are just placing the numbers at the correct coordinates on the screen to match the words on the GAME_OVER image.

The first four lines in the block above give us shots, score, hits and misses. These values are taken straight from the variables. The final screen.blit line is for the accuracy. Accuracy doesn't have its own variable but we can work out the percentage accuracy by taking the number of hits divided by the number of shots, then multiplying by 100. Just like you did in high school maths when working out percentages. Note that we're adding two strings together. The second string is just the percentage sign.

Accuracy will be written as a percentage to the nearest integer.

Integers and floats

As you probably know, an integer is a whole number. No decimal places.

As far as we're concerned here a float is a number with a decimal point. (The correct mathematical definition is a little more complex.)

If you only use integers in a sum, Python will give the answer to the nearest integer rounded down. For example, in Python, 3 divided by 4 will return 0.

Open a command prompt, load Python and try it.

-3/4 will return -1. Though 0-3/4 will return 0. (This is because of orders of operation. Python is doing 3/4 -which it rounds down to zero- and then taking that from zero.)

If you use floats in a sum, you'll get the answer as a float.

So 3.0/4 is 0.75 because by writing 3.0 we have allowed floats. Answers can be given to many significant figures, so 20/3.0 will return 6.666666666666667.

Try 0.1+0.2. The reason you get the answer you do is because computers work in binary. Storing decimals accurately isn't so easy for a machine that works in binary. We can get some unexpected, and mostly insignificant, rounding errors. Try 10.0/3

Many old space invader games gave accuracy to one decimal place. A trick to do this is to change the (100*hits/shots) sum to (1000*hits/shots)/10.)

In the sum above, (1000*hits/shots) will always return an integer because all the terms are integers.

Because (1000*hits/shots) has to be an integer, dividing by 10.0 (we can abbreviate that to 10.) will give us a float with one decimal place. This is because all the numbers after the first decimal place will be zero, in which case Python doesn't bother writing them.

If you write (100.0*hits/shots) you'll get the answer to a whole bunch decimal places.

As you will also know from your high (or is that secondary?) school maths, if you divide anything by zero you get an infinity. So if our shots are zero and we get hit, Python is going to work out that sum and get infinity. Python doesn't like infinities. It will yelp and then crash. We can fix this by replacing the final screen.blit() line, the one that deals with accuracy, with the following lines:

```
if shots == 0:
    screen.blit(font.render("--",True,(255,255,255)),(400,357))
else:
    screen.blit(font.render(str((1000*hits/shots)/10.)+"%",True,(255,
        255,255)),(400,357))
```

Now if shots equals zero, we never get to that pesky equation. Instead, Python will print the "--".

I THINK WE'RE PLAYING TOO MUCH SPACE INVADERS.

I KNOW. I'M HAVING STRANGE DREAMS.

ME TOO. I ENDLESSLY SHOOT INVADERS OUT OF THE SKY IN A GAME THAT NEVER STOPS.

WHEN I SLEEP ALL I SEE IS THE AFTERMATH OF AN APOCALYPTIC WAR. SHIVERING CHILDREN HUDDLE IN THE BURNED OUT WRECKAGE OF CRASHED FIGHTERS, SUCKING THE MARROW OUT OF THE BONES OF LONG DEAD DOGS. ZOMBIE LIKE CREATURES STALK THE DARKNESS SCREAMING FROM THE PAIN THAT RIPS THROUGH THEIR DECAYING SKIN. GRAFFITI IN STRANGE LANGUAGES APPEARS ON THE CRUMBLING WALLS BUT NOBODY EVER SEES WHO PAINTED IT. OLD MEN SHUFFLE THROUGH THE BROKEN SHELLS OF OLD CATHEDRALS BUT WHEN YOU GET CLOSE YOU SEE THEY'RE BARELY OUT OF THEIR TEENS. THE SUN IS HIDDEN BEHIND CLOUDS OF SHARP, RADIOACTIVE DUST.

OH. OKAY. MAYBE YOU SHOULD TAKE UP TENNIS OR SOMETHING

Chapter eleven

Changing the game...

Anyone for Pong?

```python
import pygame, sys
from pygame.locals import *
pygame.init()
pygame.display.set_caption("Pong")
screen = pygame.display.set_mode((1000,600))
clock = pygame.time.Clock()
ball_image = pygame.image.load("images/ball.png").convert_alpha()

class Bat:
    def __init__(self,ctrls,x):
        self.ctrls=ctrls
        self.x=x
        self.y=260

    def move(self):
        if pressed_keys[self.ctrls[0]] and self.y > 0:
            self.y -= 10
        if pressed_keys[self.ctrls[1]] and self.y < 520:
            self.y += 10

    def draw(self):
        pygame.draw.line(screen,(255,255,255),(self.x,self.y),(self.x,self.y+80),6)

class Ball:
    def __init__(self):
        self.dx=12
        self.dy=0
        self.x=475
        self.y=275

    def move(self):
        self.x +=self.dx
        self.y +=self.dy

    def draw(self):
        screen.blit(ball_image,(self.x, self.y))

ball = Ball()
bats = [ Bat( [K_a,K_z] , 10), Bat( [K_UP,K_DOWN] , 984) ]
```

```
while 1:
    clock.tick(30)
    for event in pygame.event.get():
        if event.type == QUIT:
            sys.exit()
    pressed_keys = pygame.key.get_pressed()

    screen.fill((0,0,0))

    for bat in bats:
        bat.move()
        bat.draw()

    ball.move()
    ball.draw()

    pygame.display.update()
```

What we have here is the basics of a pong game. We're going to add in a lot more features over the following pages but for now we've got bats that go up and down and a ball that launches, though it always goes in the same direction. There's no collision detection either.

Most of what we have here you'll recognise. We'll talk through stuff you haven't seen before. Then we'll get on to making the game more interesting and use some new techniques.

DO YOU WORRY PEOPLE ARE GOING TO THINK WE'RE JUST A CHEAP RIP OFF OF XKCD?

I KNOW IT'S TRUE BUT I DON'T WORRY ABOUT IT. REMEMBER, ALL THOSE PEOPLE OUT THERE, THEY'RE JUST A CHEAP RIP OFF OF GOD.

Transparency

The line below loads an image of a ball. If you look carefully you'll see it's slightly different than the lines we've used to load images of Mike, the fighter and the badguy.

```
ball_img = pygame.image.load("images/ball.png").convert_alpha()
```

The image of the ball we used has a transparent background. Not all image formats support transparency but the ball image we have used is a PNG, which does. JPEGs don't.

Using the regular **convert()** function when loading the image will show the transparent areas of an image as the original background color of the image. To solve this we use:

```
convert_alpha()
```

Note: If you use **convert_alpha()** it stops the **colorkey()** function working. So only use **convert_alpha()** when you have an image with transparent sections. Use **colorkey()** when you have a solid color your want to make transparent.

We actually downloaded an image and then gave it a transparent background in paint.net. We could have given it a color background, say red, and used the colorkey() function to make the red transparent. Either way works.

To the Bat class

Now let's look at the a Bat class. There are some new techniques being introduced here so let's just take it easy. First up, you can see we've created an __init__() function, a **move()** function and a **draw()** function. This is pretty normal. Let's look at the __init__() function.

```
def __init__(self,ctrls,x,):
    self.ctrls=ctrls
    self.x=x
    self.y=260
```

The __init__() function takes two arguments apart from self. They are **ctrls** and **x**.

Here **ctrls** is going to be a list of the keys we're going to use to control the bat. **x** is going to give the initial x position of the bat.

We can see that these arguments are then passed on to the specific instance of the bat in the next few lines. You have to do this if you're going to use those arguments in other functions in the class.

self.y has to be defined in the __init__() function but it doesn't need to take an argument because it's going to be the same for every bat.

Remember, the __init__() function only gets run once, just when an instance (a bat in this case) is created. It sets everything up to be used by the other functions.

DO YOU BELIEVE IN A GOD? A KIND OF SUPER HUMAN PROGRAMMER WHO HAS CREATED US ALL?

I DON'T KNOW. BUT I BELIEVE THIS ORANGE JUICE TASTES GOOD. APPARENTLY THE FLAVOUR WAS PROGRAMMED IN LISP.

Now let's have a look at the move() function.

```python
def move(self):
    if pressed_keys[self.ctrls[0]] and self.y >0:
        self.y -= 10
    if pressed_keys[self.ctrls[1]] and self.y <520:
        self.y += 10
```

Then we have lines that look similar to these two lines from page 89.

```python
if pressed_keys[K_LEFT] and self.x > 0:
    self.x -=3
```

The difference is what's in the square brackets of the pressed_keys[] list. **pressed_keys** is a list of all the keys that are being pressed. It's created in the game loop rather than in the move function because we might want to use it in other functions.

On page 89 we were asking if any of the keys being pressed was the left arrow (K_LEFT).

Here, in our new move() function we're asking if **self.ctrls[0]** has been pressed. So what is **self.ctrls[0]**?

We know from the **__init__()** function that **self.ctrls=ctrls**. What this is saying is that **ctrls** for this particular bat are the **ctrls** given to the bat when it was created.

If we want to understand what's going on with **ctrls** we need to look at what happens when a bat is created.

(The very observant among you might notice that pressed_keys is a variable that has been created outside the function but that the function refers to. We said on page 102 that Python doesn't do this. We said that Python needs to be told a variable is global before it goes off and finds it outside the function. There's a technical reason Python already knows **pressed_keys** is global without us having to tell it. You really don't need to know the reason but very quickly the reason is this: It's referenced before it's assigned a value. There. That wasn't too bad. It probably doesn't make too much sense but hey, just repeat the sentence and everyone will be impressed by your knowledge.)

P.S. This is also true for the **screen** and **image** variables and a few others later on.

This is how the bats are created:

```
bats = [ Bat( [K_a,K_z], 10), Bat( [K_UP,K_DOWN], 630) ]
```

The line above creates a list of bats. We're going to place it into the program after the class, where we normally place lists. Up until now we've created lists, like the missile list on page 92, and then created new objects elsewhere in the program and told Python to add them to the list. Like the lines on page 93. Here we have created a list called bats, and created two bats ourselves simply by placing them in the list.

Simplifying this line, what we have is:

```
bats = [Bat(), Bat()]
```

We have a list with two bats in it. As with the missiles, Python identifies each bat from its position in the list, so it doesn't matter if they seem to have the same name. (What we actually have there are two bat **constructors** but it's fine to think of them as the bats.)

Inside the parenthesis belonging to each bat we have placed the arguments required by the **__init__()** function. That is: **ctrls** and **x**.

ctrls is the first argument. It is a list of keys. There are just two items in the list. Then x is just a number. This will be used to for the x coordinate of a bat.

We were looking at this line:

```
if pressed_keys[self.ctrls[0]] and self.y > 0:
```

For the first condition of the if statement we're asking whether the list of pressed keys contains the key: **self.ctrls[0]** ?

The key, **self.ctrls[0]**, is the first item on the **self.ctrls[]** list. (Remember the first item on a list has the position: 0.) And the first item on that list, for the first bat, is, **K_a.** That is, the A key.

So now we're back to a line that basically says:

```
if pressed_keys[K_a] and self.y > 0:
    self.y -= 10
```

```
if pressed_keys[self.ctrls[1]] and self.y <520:
    self.y += 10
```

The second part of the move function looks for the second item in the self.ctrls list and moves the bat down. We also have the second condition in the if statement which only lets the bat move if it's above the bottom of the screen. You can see from the draw() function that the bat is 80 pixels high. The screen is 600 pixels high so if the y position of the bat is greater than 520 then it's at least partially off the screen and shouldn't be allowed to move further down.

This might all seem a bit longwinded just to get a bat to move up and down. But the great thing about classes is that once we've made a class it's easy to add instances of that class. So once we've made the first bat, making second simply means adding another bat to the list.

That's the: **Bat([K_UP,K_DOWN],630)**

And it would be easy, though a little pointless, to add more bats.

Bat([K_j,K_n],330) would add a fully working bat into the middle of the screen.

ALMOST FINISHED MY CONSTRUCTOR

Chapter twelve

A ball class...

Looking back at page 121:

```
class Ball:
    def __init__(self):
        self.dx=12
        self.dy=0
        self.x=475
        self.y=275

    def move(self):
        self.x +=self.dx
        self.y +=self.dy

    def draw(self):
        screen.blit(ball_image, self.x, self.y))
```

We've created a very basic Ball class. The __init__() function gives the ball its
position and speed. It starts in the middle of the screen and is going to be moving at
12 pixels per loop to the right. But you'll notice that because the coordinates of the
ball image are top left our coordinates are 25 pixels high and 25 pixels to the left of
the actual screen centre. The ball is 50x50 pixels so the centre of the ball will now be
at the centre of the screen.

WHO ARE YOU? I'M MIKE. I

CREATED YOU.

The move function makes the ball move. I don't think we need to say anything more about that.

The draw function blits the image. Later on we're going to doing some maths to set dx and dy. But when we do that dx and dy might be floats. This means the self.x and self.y will also become floats. Python sometimes complains if we try to place something at a coordinate denoted by floats, though not always. Just to be safe we can round a float to an integer using **int()**.

int(3.4) will return 3

So our draw() function might look like this:

```
def draw(self):
    screen.blit(ball_image,(int(self.x), int(self.y)))
```

All we've done so far very straight forward and nothing we haven't seen before. (Apart from the int() function.) But so far it would make a very boring game. We need to spice it up. But first we're going to add in the collision detection.

YOU CREATED ME?

YEAH. YOU'RE HERE TO DO ALL THE BORING STUFF WHILE I HANG OUT WITH MARTHA.

NO WAY. YOU DO THE BORING STUFF.

There are two types of collision we need to deal with. The ball needs to bounce off the top and bottom of the screen, and it needs to bounce off a bat. The first case is the easiest so let's deal with that. We did pretty much the same with bouncing the badguys off the sides of the screen.

We'll create a bounce function in the the ball class:

```
def bounce(self):
    if self.y<=0 or self.y>=550:
        self.dy *=-1
```

You can see here that if the ball touches the top or bottom of the screen we reverse dy. Set self.dy to 12 or -12 in the __init__() function and run the program and you can see it work. (Though you'll have to call the bounce() function. See page 132.)

BUT I CREATED YOU. YOU HAVE TO DO WHAT I SAY.

I CREATED THIS FOREST FIRE. THAT DOESN'T MEAN IT'S GOING TO OBEY ME.

Now for bouncing off the bats:

```
def bounce(self):
    if self.y<=0 or self.y>=550:
        self.dy *=-1

    for bat in bats:
        if pygame.Rect(bat.x,bat.y,6,80).colliderect(self.x,self.y,50,50):
            self.dx *= -1
```

The for loop goes through each bat in the list bats and runs the if statement. The if statement uses the function:

pygame.Rect().colliderect()

This function detects collisions between two rectangles. We've seen pygame.Rect() before. (Page 55) Here we're going to use it to place a rectangle over the bat that we're dealing with. We're giving **Rect()** four arguments this time. They are the x-position of the bat, the y-position of the bat, the width of the bat and the height of the bat. That is:

bat.x,bat.y,6,80

Now we have that invisible rectangle we're going to ask if it is colliding with a second rectangle. The second rectangle is described by the arguments in the colliderect() function. That is:

self.x,self.y,50,50

These arguments are the coordinates and size of the ball. If the pygame.Rect().colliderect() function detects a collision then the if statement returns a True and we reverse self.dx by multiplying it by -1. This will make the ball bounce off the bats.

Finally, don't forget to add the function call into the game loop. Like so:

```
ball.bounce()
```

This line goes in the same place we call the ball's move() and draw() functions.

Note: It doesn't matter which way round the ball and bat go. Rect() could contain the ball information and colliderect() could contain the bat information. We're in the Ball class to self is always going to refer to the ball.

I'M GOING TO CRUSH YOU INTO THE DIRT.

I'M A TEFLON COATED BATTLE TANK. I'M GOING TO GRIND YOUR BONES TO DUST.

IN YOUR DREAMS. I'M A WRECKING BALL. I'M A TWO TON TRUCK COMING RIGHT AT YOUR SKINNY FRAME.

I'M A NUKE. YOU'LL BE NOTHING BUT RADIOACTIVE VAPOUR BY THE TIME I'M FINISHED.

Those two functions, Rect() and colliderect() have the option of taking just two arguments. Rather than taking **x-postion, y-position, width, height** they can take **coordinates, size**.

This looks almost the same. In our program the colliderect() function could look like this:

```
colliderect((self.x,self,y),(50,50))
```

That's two arguments each made of a tuple. This might seem a little pointless, but Pygame has a function that will grab the size of an object.

```
get_size()
```

The line: `ball_image.get_size()` will return the tuple: (50,50)

Therefore in our program we could write:

```
colliderect((self.x,self,y),ball_image.get_size())
```

Again this might seem like more trouble than it's worth but it saves us having to look up the size of the ball if we don't know it. It also means we could change the size of the ball and not have to change the function. Soon we will see examples where the size of an object changes while the program is running. In this case **get_size()** and other similar functions are very useful.

We can't grab the size of the bat in a similar way because there is no object associated with the bat. It is just a line the Pygame constantly redraws on the fly.

Spice by numbers

The first thing we're going to do to spice up the game is launch the ball at a random angle. This is new so we'll talk you through it.

You should know that, when dealing with angles, programmers tend to use radians rather than degrees. This is because mathematicians use radians. And when it comes down to it, programming is just another branch of maths. Mathematicians aren't being malicious; at least, not in this case. Degrees work fine for measuring angles in triangles and knowing which direction to head when you're walking across the Scottish hills. But once you travel a little further, into the highlands of mathematics, radians make a lot more sense. If you want to know more there's a cute introduction here:

http://mathwithbaddrawings.com/2013/05/02/degrees-vs-radians/

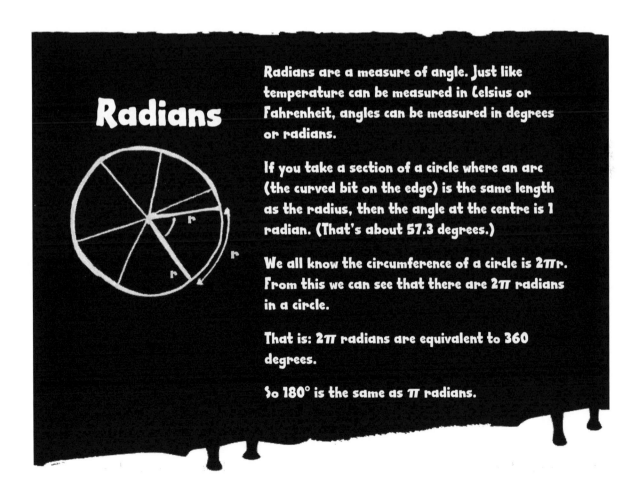

Radians

Radians are a measure of angle. Just like temperature can be measured in Celsius or Fahrenheit, angles can be measured in degrees or radians.

If you take a section of a circle where an arc (the curved bit on the edge) is the same length as the radius, then the angle at the centre is 1 radian. (That's about 57.3 degrees.)

We all know the circumference of a circle is $2\pi r$. From this we can see that there are 2π radians in a circle.

That is: 2π radians are equivalent to 360 degrees.

So 180° is the same as π radians.

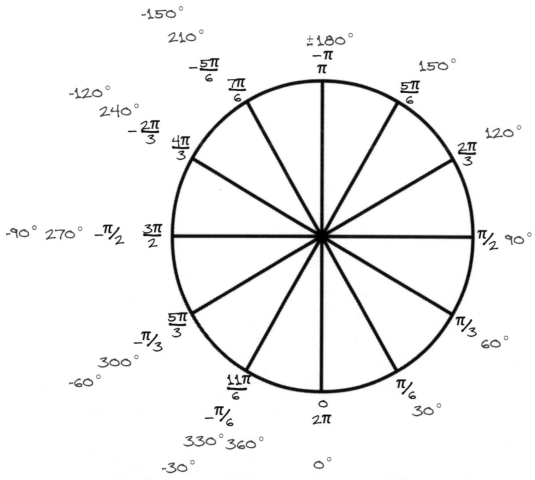

Note that each section is increasing by pi/6. We could have started at zero a gone 1/6pi, 2/6pi. 3/6pi etc. We have just simplified the fractions.

Launching a ball at a random angle

We need to rewrite the __init__() function in the ball class like this:

```
def __init__(self):
    d=((math.pi/3)*random.random()+(math.pi/3))+math.pi*random.randint(0,1)
    self.dx=math.sin(d)*12
    self.dy=math.cos(d)*12
    self.x=475
    self.y=275
```

We've used the **math** and the **random** modules from Python so we have to import these on the first line:

```
import pygame, sys, math, random
```

Now, let's look at that "d" line:

```
d=(math.pi/3)*random.random()+(math.pi/3)+math.pi*random.choice(0,1)
```

d is for direction and is going to be a the value of an angle in radians. It's not used outside the __init__() function so it doesn't need a "self".

We have to write **math.pi** rather than just **pi** because **pi** is only defined in Python's math module. This is why we loaded **math** in the first line.

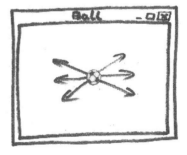

The **d** variable is going to be the angle at which the ball sets off. We want the angle to be roughly towards the left or right side of the screen, not up or down. something in this region:

136

The first bit, **math.pi/3**, give us an angle.

Remember that y is positive going down and x is positive to the right. So an angle of zero is pointing down and goes positive as it turns counter clockwise.

If we launch the ball at an angle of pi/3 this is the direction it would go:

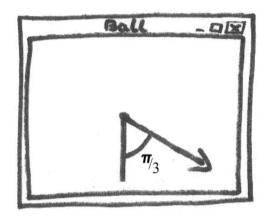

random.random() gives us a number between 0 and 1. For example, we might get 0.54 or 0.27. (Though, being python, it will be to a zillion decimal places.)

So math.pi/3*random.random() gives us an angle somewhere between 0 and pi/3 radians. (That's between 0 and 60 degrees.)

So if we launch a ball at this angle it will go somewhere in this direction:

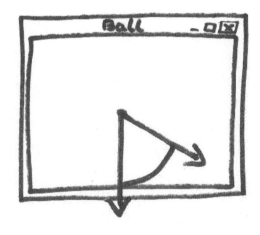

Next we add **pi/3** radians. This will shift the range of angles like so:

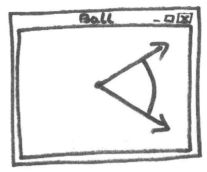

In the final part of the line the **random.choice()** function chooses a random integer from the list in the parenthesis. (We used this to randomise the speed of the badguy.) Here we are choosing from 0 or 1.

`math.pi*random.choice(0,1,)` will randomly choose either $0 \times \pi$ or $1 \times \pi$. We then add this onto the angle. (This is like adding either 0° or 180°.)

So we get an angle **d** that's somewhere in the following range:

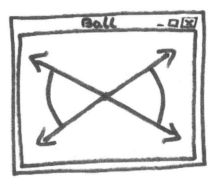

So far we haven't actually mentioned radians. We just have a number somewhere between 0 and 2π.

We want the ball to move 12 pixels in the chosen direction. But Python moves things in either the x direction or the y direction. To move at angles we have to combine the two.

```
self.dx=math.sin(d)*12
self.dy=math.cos(d)*12
```

Once we know angle d we can use **Sohcoatoa** (see page 140) to set the change in the **x** and **y** values. That is to find **dx** and **dy**.

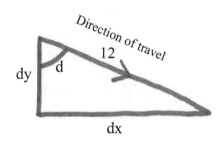

We know angle d because we've just set it. The length of the hypotenuse is the number of pixels we want the ball to move in each loop. 12 in this case.

dx is the Opposite.
dy is the Adjacent.

Here zero is pointing down. On the explanation on the opposite page zero is to the right.

dx = sin d x 12
and
dy = cos d x 12

So there we have it. We set an angle that's not completely random but has some randomness in it, then use some basic maths to work out dy and dx.

Sohcahtoa

As you may well know, or soon will if you haven't got that far at school yet, sohcoatoa is a mnemonic for the following:

For a right-angled triangle

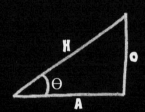

$$\sin\Theta = \frac{Opposite}{Hypotenuse} \quad \text{(that's the soh bit)}$$

$$\cos\Theta = \frac{Adjacent}{Hypotenuse} \quad \text{(that's the cah bit)}$$

We don't need the toa bit just now but you might be able to work out what $\tan\Theta$ is.

If we know angle Θ and length H (H is for Hypotenuse), then we can work out length O (O is for Opposite) and length A (A is for Adjacent).

For example:

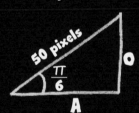

$$\sin\Theta = \frac{O}{H} \qquad \cos\Theta = \frac{A}{H}$$

$$\Rightarrow O = \sin\Theta \times H \qquad \Rightarrow A = \cos\Theta \times H$$

$$\Rightarrow O = \sin\frac{\pi}{6} \times 50 \qquad \Rightarrow A = \cos\frac{\pi}{6} \times 50$$

$$\Rightarrow O = 25 \qquad \Rightarrow A = 43.3$$

If you do this calculation on a calculator make sure it's set to use radians rather than degrees.

This code is commonly used. You'll be able to cut and paste it into other projects.

We could have used it to launch the space invaders. For example, the **__init__()** function from the badguy class on page 80 could look like this:

```
def __init__(self):
    self.x = random.randint(0,570)
    self.y = -100
    d=(math.pi/2)*random.random()-(math.pi/4)
    speed = random.randint(2,6)
    self.dx=math.sin(d)*speed
    self.dy=math.cos(d)*speed
```

(Making sure to add in **math** to the list of imports on line 1)
Try it. It works just as well as our previous method.

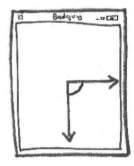

(Math.pi/2)*random.random()
gets our range of angle.
(pi/2 radians is 90°)

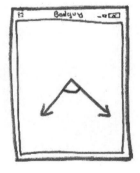

-(math.pi/4) rotates the range of angle to point down.

We're taking pi/4 radians off the angle. This effectively rotates the angle clockwise.

We set a random speed. Then we use **sohcahtoa** to find **dx** and **dy**.

We've set the starting point to to 100 pixels above the screen and a random number between 0 and 570 on the x axis.

And so, together with the **move()** and **bounce()** functions, we should get badguys coming down at random angles like this:

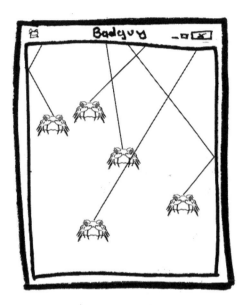

SO WHAT HAPPENED WHEN YOU COLLIDED? WE HIT EACH OTHER SO HARD WE JUST

SEEMED TO MERGE BACK INTO ONE PERSON.
SOMETHING LIKE THAT.

MY FAVOURITE THING ABOUT BEING A VIRTUAL CHARACTER IS THAT I CAN CONNECT WITH ANYTHING IN THE VIRTUAL WORLD WITH JUST A FEW LINES OF CODE. ALL OF HUMAN KNOWLEDGE IS AVAILABLE TO ME AND I HAVE NO SPATIAL OR TIME CONSTRAINTS. WHAT'S YOURS?

THAT I CAN HANG UPSIDE DOWN LIKE A BAT FOR EIGHT HOURS STRAIGHT.

Chapter thirteen

Goal scoring...

Scoring in a game of pong

First up we have to create a couple of variables to store the scores from each player. These go in the set up part of the program.

```
rscore = 0
lscore = 0
```

A goal is scored when the ball goes off the opposite side of the screen. When this happens we need to add 1 to the player's score and reset the ball to middle, where it's launched again.

Place the following code in the game loop after the ball's function calls. Check in the appendix or on the website if you're not exactly sure where.

```
if ball.x < -50:
    ball=Ball()
    rscore+=1

if ball.x > 1000:
    ball=Ball()
    lscore+=1
```

Here you can see that if the ball goes off the left hand side of the screen (that is, if **ball.x** is less than -50) then Python with run a line:

```
ball=Ball()
```

We used this technique to create a new badguy on page 79. The line creates an instance of the ball class and runs the **__init__()** function in that class. That is, it creates a ball. But we can only have one ball so the variable **ball** is pointed at the data for the new ball, and the old ball (by that we mean the data for the old ball) is cleaned up by Python's garbage clearing system. (Python really does have garbage collection.)

Right after that we add 1 to the **rscore**. **rscore** and **lscore** are created in the setup part of the program because they're used here in the game loop as well as the Ball class. They can't be created in the game loop because they'd be reset to zero with every loop.

The second block of three lines work in a similar way for the ball going off the right hand side of the screen.

Next we'll put those scores on the screen. Again, we've done this before.

We create a font variable in that first section of the program.

```
font = pygame.font.Font(None,40)
```

Then, last thing before the screen.update() in the game loop, we add the lines that blit the score to the screen.

```
txt = font.render(str(lscore),True,(255,255,255))
screen.blit(txt,(20,20))
txt = font.render(str(rscore),True,(255,255,255))
screen.blit(txt,(980-txt.get_width(),20))
```

You can see we've written these lines slightly differently to the lines we wrote on page 117 that blitted the scores for the space invader game. Looking carefully we can see that functionally they do the exact same thing. Here we have created a variable called **txt** -it doesn't matter that we reuse it on line 3 because by then its line 1 stuff is complete- and given it some attributes. We've then blitted **txt** to a particular coordinate using screen.blit(). On page 117 we wrote the attributes straight into the screen.blit() function. Either way is fine, but we have a good reason for doing it this way here.

If you look at the last line we've defined the x-postion in the screen.blit() function as:

$$980-txt.get\_width()$$

As you might guess the **get_width()** function fetches the width of something. We're using **get_width()** because we want to be neat on the screen.

We want to put the right hand edge of the right hand score (stored in the **txt** variable) 20 pixels from the edge of the screen. This is easy for the left hand score, but the right hand score gives us a problem. The score's coordinate is top left. So the x-position will be 980 pixels (that's the width of the screen minus the 20 pixels) minus the width of the score.

The width of score will change as the score increases. 8 is wider than 1. 1000 is wider than 100.

get_width() solves this problem. It measures the width of score at any point in time and we can use this value to position the score correctly.

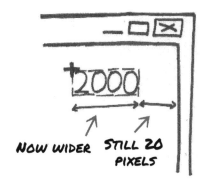

NOW WIDER — STILL 20 PIXELS

WE'RE CONSTANTLY MEASURED AND ANALYSED. THIS PERCENTAGE, THAT MARK. RATED AND RANKED ACCORDING TO OUR ABILITIES AND THE WHIMS OF OUR ELDERS, LEADERS AND PEERS. WE'RE ONE WALKING MASS OF STATISTICS. BUT LIFE ISN'T ABOUT NUMBERS. IT'S ABOUT THE FEELING OF THE SUNSHINE ON YOUR FACE, THE THRILL OF RUNNING FAST DOWN HILL. THE SOUNDS OUR HEARTS MAKE WHEN WE LIE NEXT TO EACH OTHER.

SO WHAT DO THINK OF THE GAME?

83%

We could have used the **get_width** function in other places. For example, in the space invader game we added a missile to the missiles list with the following line:

```
missiles.append(Missile(self.x+50))
```

That **(self.x+50)** is the position of the middle of the fighter. We happen to know the fighter is 100 pixels wide. But if we couldn't be bothered looking it up, or if we had several fighters of different widths, we could have written:

```
missiles.append(Missile(self.x+fighter_image.get_width()/2))
```

Similarly, when setting the y-position of the fighter we wrote:

```
screen.blit(fighter_image,(self.x,591))
```

But we had to work out that 591 by looking up the height of the screen and taking away the height of the fighter. We could have let Python do the maths with:

```
screen.blit(fighter_image,(self.x, screen.get_height()-
                    fighter_image.get_height()))
```

The line we just wrote to blit the right hand score could look like this:

```
screen.blit(txt,(screen.get_width()-20-txt.get_width(),20))
```

YOU WERE GOING TO MEET ME AT THE PARK. WE HAD A TENNIS MATCH ARRANGED.

I GOT INTO BUILDING A DIARY APP. I TOTALLY FORGOT.

IT'S OKAY. I PLAYED WITH SOMEONE ELSE. WE FOUND THIS GLITCH.

Sometimes the ball hits a bat and bounces but in the next game loop, because the bat is moving, the ball and bat are still touching. Then the bounce function kicks in again and bounces the ball.

If you haven't seen this glitch try hitting the ball with the very end of the bat while the bat is moving. Once in a while the ball will get caught on the bat.

What happens is something like this:

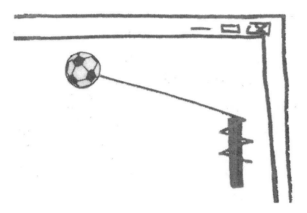

There are several ways to fix this glitch. We've decided to make it so the ball will only bounce if it's travelling towards the bat. If the ball has bounced once and is travelling away from the bat but is still overlapping the bat a little, we won't let it bounce.

We do this by working out the direction the ball is travelling in. Well, we know if **dx** is positive then the ball is travelling to the right. A negative **dx** means the ball is travelling to the left.

We can say: If the ball is moving to the right and it hits the bat on the right then it's allowed to bounce. If it's travelling to the left and hits the bat to the left then it can bounce. Otherwise, carry on moving as before.

To make this happen we're going to mark the bats as either left or right. In fact, we're going to mark them as either 1 or -1. 1 for right and -1 for left.

```
def __init__(self,ctrls,x,side):
```

First we'll add **side** to the arguments taken by the bat's __init__() function.

Now the __init__() function is asking for three arguments. And here is where they're given:

```
bats = [Bat([K_a,K_z],10,-1), Bat([K_UP,K_DOWN],984,1)]
```

You can see the bat on the left side, with a **x** value of 10, gives a **side** value of -1. The right hand bat, with 984 for it's **x** value, gives 1 for its **side** value.

Now update the Bat class's __init__() function so the **side** value is passed on.

```
def __init__(self,ctrls,x,side):
    self.ctrls=ctrls
    self.x=x
    self.y=260
    self.side=side
```

We're also going to add a condition in the Ball's bounce function. Like so:

```
def bounce(self):
    if self.y<=0  or self.y>=550:
        self.dy *=-1

    for bat in bats:
        if pygame.Rect(bat.x,bat.y,6,80).colliderect(self.x,self.y,50,50)
            and abs(self.dx)/self.dx == bat.side:
            self.dx *= -1
```

Now we have a second condition that has to be met before self.dx gets multiplied by -1.

abs(self.dx)/self.dx must be equal to **bat.side**

The **abs()** function gives you the **absolute** of any number. That is it turns all numbers into positive numbers. For example, -6 would become 6. But 6 would remain as 6.

If you take the absolute of a number and divide it by the original number, you're going to get an answer of either -1 or 1. For example, the absolute of -6 divided by -6 is 6/-6, which is -1. The absolute of 9 divided by 9 is 9/9 which is 1.

`abs(self.dx)/self.dx`, gives the direction the ball is going in as either 1 or -1.

A ball with a negative **dx** will return -1. A positive **dx** will return 1.

The bat on the right, with a x-position of 984, was given a **side** value of 1. The ball on the left was given a **side** value of -1. So the final condition asks if the direction of the ball is equal to the **side** value of the ball. Only if that's true can we bounce.

THE GAME WORKS BETTER NOW.

Anna?

GREAT. THANKS. ANNA WILL BE PLEASED. THE WAY THE BALL STUCK TO HER RACKET WAS KIND OF WEIRD.

Glitches like the one we've just solved come up all the time. You write some code that you think will do something, but some tiny little other thing bugs it out. Solving these glitches is something you have to get creative with. You should expect glitches and, rather than get frustrated, see them as an interesting challenge. (Or though, of course, frustration is more normal.)

Pitch Markings

We're going to add in a centre line and a centre circle to the pong pitch.

```
pygame.draw.line(screen,(255,255,255),(screen.get_width()/2,0),
    (screen.get_width()/2,screen.get_height()),3)
pygame.draw.circle(screen,(255,255,255),(screen.get_width()/2,
    screen.get_height()/2),50,3)
```

We've drawn circles and lines before, way back on pages 14 and 27. Both the **line()** function and **circle()** function take five arguments. These lines need to be placed immediately after the **screen.fill()** line in the program. We need them to be laid over the screen fill but under the ball.

We've used the **get.width()** and **get.height()** functions rather than work out the numbers ourselves. Another advantage of this method is that if you change the dimensions of the screen, the positions of the objects on the screen will be automatically corrected.

We will just look at the third and forth arguments in the **line()** function. The third argument is the coordinates of the beginning of the line. The x-position is `screen.get_width()/2`which will give us half way across the screen. The y-position is 0. In the fourth argument, the end of the line, we have the same x-position but we've given the y-position as the height of the screen. Hence, we get a line that goes straight down the middle of the screen regardless of the screen size.

With the circles you just need to remember the coordinates of a circle mark the centre of a circle, not the top left.

HEY, MARTHA. THIS IS ANNA.

Hi, Martha. Wow, you're so brave wearing those boots with that skirt. Love it.

!

WE LIVE IN BEAUTIFUL UNIVERSE.

WE SURELY DO. YOU KNOW, IT'S BEEN A LONG
DAY. I THINK I NEED TO GET SOME SLEEP.

ARE YOU KIDDING? PROGRAMMERS DON'T
SLEEP. SOMETIMES WE PRETEND TO SLEEP
JUST SO OTHER PEOPLE DON'T GET TOO
INTIMIDATED BY US BUT REALLY WE JUST LIE
IN THE DARK FIGURING OUT STUFF. THANK GOD FOR THAT. I THOUGHT I WAS GOING
TO HAVE TO WASTE THE NEXT EIGHT HOURS.
WHAT'S NEXT?

Chapter fourteen

The randomiser...

Updating d, dy and dx

Another obvious thing to do is add some variation to how the ball bounces off the bat. At the moment the ball bounces perfectly and always at the same speed. This makes the game play quite predictable.

We described the bounce() function in the ball class on page 131. The if statement detects if the ball is touching the top or bottom of the screen and if it is, it reverses **dy**. Then there is a for loop that detects if the the ball is touching a bat and, if it is, it reverses **dx**.

If we're going to randomise the angle that means messing with **d**. We originally launched the ball at angle **d** but after the ball bounces it is no longer travelling in direction **d**. The ball has now changed angle but **d** hasn't. If we're going to randomise the angle the ball bounces off the bat so it's important we have the correct angle at which it hits the bat. Fortunately for us there is a cute maths function, **math.atan2()**, that will take **dx** and **dy** and tell you the angle **d**. So you kind of work backwards to work out the new value of **d**.

We're going to add this into the **bounce()** function, like this:

```
def bounce(self):
    if self.y <= 0 or self.y >= 550:
        self.dy *= -1
        self.d = math.atan2(self.dx,self.dy)
```

You'll notice that we've changed **d** to **self.d**. Up until now we've only used **d** in the **__init__()** function. Now we're going to use it here in the **bounce()** function we need to go back to the **__init_()** function and change all the **d**s to **self.d**. (There are three of them.)

In summary, when the ball bounces off the top or bottom of the screen, **dy** reverses and we recalculate **d**.

WHAT DOES "EXTERNAL PROTOCOL ERROR" MEAN?

IT MEANS THE WRONG PERSON'S SITTING IN FRONT OF THE COMPUTER.

Now we have an accurate **d** we can bounce the ball off the bat in a slightly different way. If we look back at the diagram on page 135 we can see that if we multiply the angle by -1 it does exactly the same thing as multiplying **dx** by -1. Imagine you're travelling away from the centre of the circle and your angle gets multiplied by -1. It's like bouncing off a vertical wall or bat.

This is why it was important for us to have the correct angle. Now change the for loop in the bounce() function (page 150) to look like this:

```
for bat in bats:
    if pygame.Rect(bat.x,bat.y,6,80).colliderect(self.x,self.y,50,50)
        and abs(self.dx)/self.dx == bat.side:
            self.d *= -1
```

We've changed **self.d** so we need to update **dx** and **dy**. If we don't, dx and dy will stay at their old values even though self.d has changed, meaning the ball will just keeping going rather than bounce. So we have to add two lines at the bottom of the **for loop**. Now the complete bounce() function will look like this:

```
def bounce(self):
    if self.y<=0  or self.y>=550:
        self.dy *=-1
        self.d = math.atan2(self.dx,self.dy)

    for bat in bats:
        if pygame.Rect(bat.x,bat.y,6,80).colliderect(self.x,self.y,50,50)
            and abs(self.dx)/self.dx == bat.side:
            self.d *= -1
            self.dx=math.sin(self.d)*12
            self.dy=math.cos(self.d)*12
```

Now we have a **bounce()** function that works and our variables, **dx**, **dy** and **d** are all kept up to date.

Random angles

Now we can randomise **self.d**, making the bounce off the bat less predictable.

```
for bat in bats:
        if (pygame.Rect(bat.x,bat.y,6,80).colliderect(self.x,self.y,50,50)
            and abs(self.dx)/self.dx == bat.side):
            self.d += random.random()*math.pi/4 -math.pi/8
            self.d *= -1
            self.dx=math.sin(self.d)*12
            self.dy=math.cos(self.d)*12
```

The highlighted line works in the same way we've seen for similar lines before. **random.random()*math.pi/4** gives us a random angle in the range **0** to **π/4**. By taking away **π/8** we shift that angle to somewhere in the **-π/8** to **π/8** range. (That's -22.5° to 22.5°.) We then add that random angle to **self.d**, making it go up or down just a little bit.

Adding some randomness to the angle is good, but it causes us a problem. This often happens when programming. You add a feature and then discover a bunch of unintended consequences. Here we have the possibility of the angle becoming so steep that the ball mostly goes up and down the screen and hardly goes sideways at all. What we need is a way of limiting the angle.

I HAVE A RANDOMISER GUN.

NO! DON'T!

MIKE! NO!

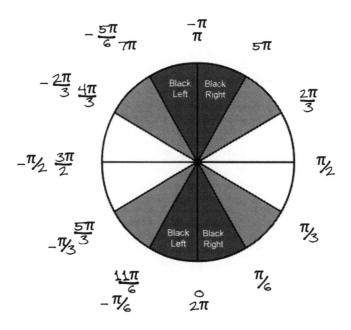

Looking at the wagon wheel above, the ball gets launched somewhere in the white section. After that, the randomising of **self.d** could potentially push it's angle of movement into the grey and black sections. We don't mind the grey, the ball is still going to zig-zag across the screen at a fair rate. But if **self.d** gets into the black zone then that's a problem. So we're going to write some code that basically says: if in black zone, go back to white zone.

THE FIRST RULE OF USING A WEAPON IS
KNOWING WHICH END IS THE NASTY END.

Here's the code to set the limits on the angle the ball can travel:

```
for bat in bats:
    if (pygame.Rect(bat.x,bat.y,6,80).colliderect(self.x,self.y,50,50) and
        abs(self.dx)/self.dx == bat.side):
        self.d+= random.random()*math.pi/4 -math.pi/8
        if (0 < self.d < math.pi/6) or (math.pi*5/6 < self.d < math.pi):
            self.d=((math.pi/3)*random.random()+(math.pi/3))
        elif (math.pi < self.d < math.pi*7/6) or (math.pi*11/6 < self.d < math.pi*2):
            self.d=((math.pi/3)*random.random()+(math.pi/3))+math.pi
        self.d*=-1
        self.d%=math.pi*2

        self.dx=math.sin(self.d)*12
        self.dy=math.cos(self.d)*12
```

It looks pretty complicated but once you get the hang of it it's not so complicated.
Here's the pseudo code:

FOR ANY BAT THE BALL COULD HIT:
    IF THE BALL IS HITTING A BAT AND GOING TOWARDS THE BAT
        CHANGE THE ANGLE (d) THE BALL IS MOVING AT BY A LITTLE
        IF THE NEW ANGLE IS TOO STEEP TO THE RIGHT
            SET d TO A SHALLOW ANGLE TO THE RIGHT
        OR ELSE IF THE ANGLE IS TOO STEEP TO THE LEFT
            SET d TO A SHALLOW ANGLE TO THE LEFT
        MULTIPLY d BY-1
        MAKE THE ANGLE A POSITIVE VALUE

        RESET dx
        RESET dy

On that first highlighted line we're checking to see if self.d is between **0** and **π/6** or between **5π/6** and **π**. That is, is it in the "black right" zones on page 159? If this returns a True then on the next line we set self.d to somewhere in the right hand white zone. This line is taken from the original ball launch code from page 136. It doesn't have the **pi*randon.randint(0,1)** added onto the end because we only want the ball to move to the right.

The **elif** line detects balls in the "black left" sections and resets them to the "left white" section. We do add pi at the end of the forth highlighted line because that's how we make the ball go left. (It's like adding 180°.)

But we still have a problem. If you take the angle that's at "10 o'clock" on the diagram on page 135 you can see it can be called either **4π/3** or **-2π/3**. They mean the same thing. Our program sometimes uses the first version, like when it originally launches the ball, and sometimes uses the second, like if the ball is heading in the direction **2π/3** and we bounce it off the right hand bat. In this case we multiply the angle by -1, giving us **-2π/3**.

But in the code we've just written we only detect the black zones using the **4π/3** version. For the whole of the left hand side of the wagon wheel it only uses the positive values, never the negatives. Negatives would mess it up.

So we use this line: `self.d%=math.pi*2`

You can see it in the code on the previous page. The line converts the negative values to the corresponding positive values. That % sign stands for **modulus**. Here **modulus** basically converts any angle to its distance from zero in the positive direction. If your angle is negative it works out the positive equivalent. If your angle goes above **2π** (360°) then the modulus will start at zero again -this is the math.pi*2 bit in the equation above. So the **modulus** of the angle **3π** is **π**. The **modulus** of **-3π** is also **π**.

It doesn't really matter if you don't immediately understand this; the point is, it fixes our problem.

Now we have some randomness, but not so much that it ruins the game.

THEN THE DRAGON RANDOMLY TURNED INTO A SMALL CAT. AND IT DIDN'T MATTER I WAS UP IN THE AIR BECAUSE THERE DOESN'T SEEM TO BE ANY GRAVITY AROUND HERE ANYWAY.

I NOTICED WE'RE NOT FALLING DOWN EVEN THOUGH THERE'S NO GROUND BENEATH US. WE'LL SORT THAT IN THE NEXT BOOK I EXPECT.

The need for speed

Another obvious change we going to make to the game is to speed up the ball every time it hits a bat. For this we're going to have to add a **speed** variable into the **__init__**() function of the Ball class:

```
def __init__(self):
    self.d=((math.pi/3)*random.random()+(math.pi/3))+
            math.pi*random.randint(0,1)
    self.speed = 12
    self.dx=math.sin(self.d)*self.speed
    self.dy=math.cos(self.d)*self.speed
    self.x=475
    self.y=275
```

Note that we have to create self.speed before we use it in the dx and dy lines. You can't refer to a variable before you have created it.

In the **bounce**() function we need to add in the lines highlighted in dark grey below. If a ball hits a bat we multiply self.speed by 1.1. However, we're only doing this if the speed is less than 20. 20 is the speed limit.

```
def bounce(self):
    if (self.y<=0 and self.dy < 0) or (self.y>=550 and self.dy > 0):
        self.dy *= -1
        self.d=math.atan2(self.dx,self.dy)

    for bat in bats:
        if (pygame.Rect(bat.x,bat.y,6,80).colliderect(self.x,self.y,50,50) and
            abs(self.dx)/self.dx == bat.side):
            self.d+= random.random()*math.pi/4 -math.pi/8
            if (0 < self.d < math.pi/6) or (math.pi*5/6 < self.d < math.pi):
                self.d=((math.pi/3)*random.random()+(math.pi/3))
            elif (math.pi < self.d < math.pi*7/6) or (math.pi*11/6 < self.d < math.pi*2):
                self.d=((math.pi/3)*random.random()+(math.pi/3))+math.pi
            self.d*=-1
            self.d%=math.pi*2

            if self.speed < 20:
                self.speed *=1.1

            self.dx=math.sin(self.d)*self.speed
            self.dy=math.cos(self.d)*self.speed
```

162

Bop the ball

Now an alternative way to speed up the ball. Rather than have the ball accelerate automatically every time it hits a bat, we're going to make the players hit the ball with the bat. You're going to hit a key, the bat will zing forward a little and bop the ball, giving it a speed boast.

So first, let's get the bats working. On a key press, let's make it Q for the left hand player and the right hand shift key for the right hand player, the bat will jump 10 pixels towards the centre of the screen for a short time, let's make it 5 hundredths of a second, and back again.

First we're going to create a variable in the Bat class to record the time the last bop began. We'll call it **lastbop**. This can be created inside the class because it will never be used outside the class.

```
class Bat:
    def __init__(self,ctrls,x,side):
        self.ctrls=ctrls
        self.x=x
        self.y=260
        self.side=side
        self.lastbop = 0
```

Then we're going to create a **bop()** function:

```
def bop(self):
    if time.time() > self.lastbop + 0.3:
        self.lastbop = time.time()
```

The **bop()** function sets the time of the last bop. It also prevents us from updating **lastbop** more than once every 0.3 of a second. We're going to use this to stop a player constantly bopping. If they could then bopping the ball would be too easy.

Make sure you add the **time** module on the first line of the program.

When the game first starts **lastbop** will equal zero. When the **bop()** function is called the if statement will return a True and **lastbop** will be set to the current time. If the function is called at any time in the next 0.3 of a second then the if statement will return a False and **lastbop** won't be updated. After 0.3 seconds has passed the if statement can return a True and we can get a new time for **lastbop**.

Now let's see how we use **lastbop**.

```
def draw(self):
    offset = -self.side*(time.time() < self.lastbop+0.05)*10
    pygame.draw.line(screen,(255,255,255),(self.x+offset,self.y),
            (self.x+offset,self.y+80),6)
```

We've introduced a variable called **offset** into the **draw()** function. First let's look at what **offset** does when the line is actually drawn. That's the third line above. It gets added to self.x. So it's going to shift the bat sideways.

When right hand player bops, the right hand bat needs to be shifted 10 pixels to the left. Likewise, when the left hand player bops, the left hand bat needs to be shifted 10 pixels to the right.

We can see the code where the **bop()** function is called on page 167. The function will be called for a particular bat depending on which trigger key has been pressed.

Looking at where **offset** is created, on the second line above, you can see its value is decided by three values multiplied together. The first is **-self.side**. For the left hand bat **self.side** is equal to -1 and for the right hand bat **self.side** equals 1. (We can see this from the line in which the bats are created on page 150). So for the left bat we're multiplying by 1 (that's minus minus one) and for the right bat we're multiplying by -1. This gives us the direction the bat is going to move when we bop.

The last value is 10. This gives us how far the bat is going to move.

The middle value is a bit strange. We have:

$$(\texttt{time.time() < self.lastbop + 0.05})$$

This is a statement that's going to return a **True** or a **False**. It's going to return a **True** for 0.05 seconds after **lastbop** was set to **time.time()**, which happened when the **bop()** function was called, which in turn happened when the trigger key was pressed. Once 0.05 seconds has passed then it will return a **False**.

Well, remember from page 45 that we said **True** is the same as **1** and **False** is the same as **0**.

So if the left hand bat calls the function, for 0.05 seconds **offset** will be equal to 1x1x10. For the right hand bat **offset** will be equal to -1x1x10.

After that the middle value will become a zero, meaning for both bats the offset will become zero.

Here we have some code that will make something briefly jump. Like a quick piston. If you were just using one bat then it could be simplified. They'd be no self.side to deal with. It's worth reading through this code a few times and properly understanding it because you'll be able to use it in many different situations.

Using True and False statements mathematically

We have said that Python treats True as equivalent to 1 and False as equivalent to 0.

To prove this let's try adding two True statements together. Open a command line, load up Python and simply add two true statements together. We've done (2<3) + (8>4). Python has returned an answer of 2.

```
C:\Windows\System32\cmd.exe - python                    —  □  ✕

Microsoft Windows [Version 6.3.9600]
(c) 2013 Microsoft Corporation. All rights reserved.

C:\Windows\System32>python
Python 2.7.3 (default, Apr 10 2012, 23:31:26) [MSC v.1500 32 bit (Intel)] on win
32
Type "help", "copyright", "credits" or "license" for more information.
>>> (2<3) + (8>4)
2
>>>
```

Try something like: (True+True+True)**2

Or: False * 82

Or: (2>9) * 10

Remember that True and False have a capital first letter

Making the bop work.

On page 162 we inserted the following two lines in the for loop in the bounce() function:

```
if self.speed < 20:
        self.speed *=1.1
```

When a collision between the bat and the ball is detected, these lines multiply the speed by 1.1 until the speed reaches 20.

We're going to replace these lines with the following:

```
if time.time() < bat.lastbop + 0.05:
    self.speed *= 1.5
```

Here we're saying that if the bop has been called in the last 5 hundredths of a second then multiply the speed by 1.5. It takes a little practice to do this in the game but we figure 5 hundredths is about right. You could of course make it easier to bop the ball by increasing the 0.05 to something like 0.1.

You could also add in a speed limit by making that first line:

```
if time.time() < bat.lastbop + 0.05 and self.speed < 20:
    self.speed *= 1.5
```

You know how to show a woman a good time, right?

I WAS KINDA HOPING YOU CAME WITH TECH SUPPORT.

And finally we have to call the bop() function. As we said earlier, we're going to use the **Q** and the **Right Shift** keys to initiate a bop. This is going to be done in the for loop that contains the quit section in much the same way we created the fire button for the missiles on page 94.

```
for event in pygame.event.get():
    if event.type == QUIT:
        sys.exit()
    if event.type == KEYDOWN:
        if event.key == K_q:
            bats[0].bop()
        if event.key == K_RSHIFT:
            bats[1].bop()
pressed_keys = pygame.key.get_pressed()
```

On page 94 we were only looking for one possible key press (space) and there was only one possible result (call the fire() function). Here we have two possible inputs and two possible outcomes so we've had to use two if statements inside the if statement that looks for the **KEYDOWN** event.

WHEN GHOSTS DISCOVER TIME
TRAVEL IT'S GOING TO BE SO
MUCH FUN HAUNTING MYSELF.

There is another glitch we have found. Sometimes the ball can get stuck to the top or bottom of the screen in much the same way it got stuck to the bats, as described on page 149. This only happens when the ball bounces off a bat and immediately touches the top or bottom edge of the screen. The program will detect the ball touching the top or bottom, but if the random bounce has reduced self.d then the ball won't move completely off the top or bottom of the screen on the next loop. It will then try and bounce again. To fix this we are only going to allow the ball to bounce if it's travelling towards the edge (top or bottom) it has just hit. This is highlighted in light grey on page 162. Now the ball only bounces if it's touching the top edge and heading up   (ie: dy < 0) or touching the bottom edge and heading down (ie: dy > 0).

As is normal, we have built a program that has developed some bugs along the way. Very little you write will work first time; and the better you get at programming the more this is going to be true.

WHAT DID YOU SAY YOU
WERE DOING?

Just fixing some glitches.

RELATIONSHIPS.

INPUTS:OUTPUTS:

Be kind and do
what she wants.

She'll call
you a loser.

Treat her mean.

She'll love
you forever.

Chapter fifteen

A different game over screen...

A different game over screen

Now we're going to add in a game over screen. This time, rather than create an image and then blitting the scores over the top of that image, we're going to write the words and scores straight onto the screen. This can often be a better option because it means storing fewer of those memory sapping images. For a game like this saving memory doesn't matter, but there might be situations where it does.

Our final screen will look something like this:

We've added in the word "score" twice in pink. Our black and white book isn't showing this but the code we've used writes in pink. Then we've printed the final scores under the words. You, of course, can do something more extravagant if you want.

First of all we need to create the two new fonts we're going to use. These lines go in the setup part of the program, right where we created our first font.

```
font2 = pygame.font.SysFont("corbel",70)
font3 = pygame.font.Font(None,60)
```

font2 uses the system font **corbel**. And we've set its size to 70. **font3** is just the default font again but we've set the size to 60.

Variables like theses go in the setup because they're used in the game loop but they don't change in every game loop. In fact, these variables never change at all. For now the same is true of variables like screen, clock and the images.

Here's the code we're going to place in the game loop.

```
if rscore > 9 or lscore > 9:

        txt = font2.render("score",True,(255,0,255))
        screen.blit(txt,(screen.get_width()/4 - txt.get_width()/2,
            screen.get_height()/4))
        screen.blit(txt,(screen.get_width()*3/4 - txt.get_width()/2,
            screen.get_height()/4))
        txt = font3.render(str(lscore),True,(255,255,255))
        screen.blit(txt,(screen.get_width()/4 - txt.get_width()/2,
            screen.get_height()/2))
        txt = font3.render(str(rscore),True,(255,255,255))
        screen.blit(txt,(screen.get_width()*3/4 - txt.get_width()/2,
            screen.get_height()/2))

        while 1:
            for event in pygame.event.get():
                if event.type == QUIT:
                    sys.exit()

            pygame.display.update()
```

This isn't the easiest code to read but take it easy and it will make sense. We will go through the code over the following few pages. This chunk of code needs to go before the display.update() in the game loop. Now there will be two display updates; one in the main game loop and one here.

WHICH IS GREATER THAN WHICH?

LET'S PLAY GAMES TOGETHER AND LAUGH LOTS.

Let's create our own fashion line and make a million bucks.

First to 10

There are several things we need to do before our game over screen is needed. First we need something that will trigger the end of the game.

```
if rscore > 9 or lscore > 9:
```

We've decided the winner is the first to ten. The line above returns a true when either player scores over 9. So once either of the scores hit ten we blit some text onto the screen.

Again we've used that **txt** variable over and over, which is okay because we keep redefining it.

```
txt = font2.render("score",True,(255,0,255))
```

Here we're using the second font we created. We're rendering the word "score" and giving it a color. "score" is a string; it has nothing to do with our score variables. We're just going to blit the word score onto the screen.

```
screen.blit(txt,(screen.get_width()/4 - txt.get_width()/2, screen.get_height()/4))
screen.blit(txt,(screen.get_width()*3/4 -txt.get_width()/2, screen.get_height()/4))
```

Screen.blit() takes its usual two arguments. First is the object to blit, which is the contents of the txt variable, then the coordinates of where to blit to.

The x-position in the first line is `screen.get_width()/4 - txt.get_width()/2`

This will place the word "score" a quarter of the way across the screen. The second line places "score" three quarters of the way across the screen. The y-position is a quarter of the way down the screen except we haven't bothered to minus half the height of **txt** so it's the top of the word "score" rather than the middle that's exactly a quarter of the way down the screen.

I can see you like him but this is a game I'm going to win.

173

```
txt = font3.render(str(lscore),True,(255,255,255))
screen.blit(txt,(screen.get_width()/4 - txt.get_width()/2,screen.get_height()/2))
txt = font3.render(str(rscore),True,(255,255,255))
screen.blit(txt,(screen.get_width()*3/4 - txt.get_width()/2,screen.get_height()/2))
```

Then we have the lines that render and blit the **lscore** and **rscore** variables using the third font we created. You should be able to work out what's going on here. It's pretty much the same as the previous page.

```
while 1:
    for event in pygame.event.get():
        if event.type == QUIT:
            sys.exit()

    pygame.display.update()
```

You've seen this before back on page 111. We're now stuck in a loop. We will show you how to get out of this loop and restart the game without having to quit the whole program on page 180.

So now when the the game is won a game over screen appears and the ball and bats freeze.

DEAR MIKE.

ANNA IS SO CONTROLLING AND EVIL. YOU
JUST CAN'T SEE IT BECAUSE YOU'RE...

Martha begins a letter to Mike but then has a better idea.

Countdown

An alternative to the "first to ten" method might be to set a time. This would be easy. Make sure you've imported **time** in that first line of the program. We create a variable called **match_start** to store the time at the beginning of the game. This can go in the variable list at the top of the program.

```
match_start = time.time()
```

Instead of the line:

```
if rscore > 9 or lscore > 9:
```

Use:

```
if time.time()- match_start > 60:
```

After 60 seconds this line will return a true and the game will be over. This is because **match_start** is set to the same value as **time.time()** when the game starts. **time.time()** increases by 1 every second so after 60 seconds **time.time()** will be 60 higher than **match_start** and we'll get a True.

MARTHA, WE'RE GOING TO GO
SKATING AND MAYBE HAVE PIZZA
AFTER. YOU WANT TO COME?

I... I NEED TO GET THIS
PROJECT FINISHED.

See you tomorrow, Martha.

An on screen clock

We could also easily place the clock on the screen. These lines would go after the pitch marking lines towards the beginning of the game loop.

```
txt = font.render(str(int(time.time() - match_start)),True,(255,255,255))
screen.blit(txt,(screen.get_width()/2 -txt.get_width()/2,20))
```

We're starting here with **time.time() - match_start**. This gives us the time since the program was launched. We turn it into an integer using **int()**, then turn that integer into a string using **str()**. We then render this in the font we created earlier and call the whole thing **txt.**

The second line then blits **txt** in the centre of the screen on the x-axis, remembering to shift **txt** half its width to the left so it's properly centred, and 20 pixels down on the y axis.

We could also go to the line of code that creates the centre line running down the middle of the screen (page 152) and start it 50 pixels lower so it doesn't overlap with the clock display. And place a box around the clock (we'll leave this to you, though it is shown in the code on the website.)

If you want time to count down instead of up then replace:

```
time.time() - match_start
```

With:

```
60-(time.time() - match_start)
```

NOW LET'S SEE WHO'S GOING TO WIN.

GLAD I CAN PROGRAM
A RESET LEVER.

Chapter sixteen

Restarting the game...

WOAH!

I FEEL LIKE THIS HAS
HAPPENED BEFORE

Restarting with a key press

While we're writing text onto the screen, there's something else we need. That's a way of restarting the game. We want to be able to press a key and play again. So let's make the space key our restart. We create another font up at the top of the program -it's just a different size the others.

```
font4 = pygame.font.Font(None,30)
```

Then we add two further lines of code under the similar lines from page 172.

```
txt = font4.render("Press Space to restart",True,(255,255,255))
screen.blit(txt,(screen.get_width()*5/9,screen.get_height()-50))
```

We've rendered some text and placed it on the screen five ninths of the way across and 50 pixels from the bottom. The text says: **Press Space to restart**. It's placed in quotes to make it a **string**.

We finished the game by jumping into the while loop that just keeps looping until we quit using the ✕ . You might remember from page 99 that we can also escape a loop using a **break statement**. So when we hit space we want to trigger a **break** in the loop that we're caught inside.

```
while 1:
    for event in pygame.event.get():
        if event.type == QUIT:
            sys.exit()
        pressed_keys = pygame.key.get_pressed()
        if pressed_keys[K_SPACE]:
            break
    pygame.display.update()
```

We have to add in the line:

pressed_keys = pygame.key.get_pressed()

because, with us trapped in this little loop, it's no longer happening in the main part of the game loop. The next line detects if an item on our pressed_keys list is the SPACE key. If it is, then the **break** kicks in, pushing us back into the game loop.

But we have a problem. A player still has 10 goals, or the clock has gone over 60, so the game loop will put us straight back into the game over section. We'll find ourselves back in that little loop. So we have to reset all the game variables before we break out of that loop.

```python
while 1:
    for event in pygame.event.get():
        if event.type == QUIT:
            sys.exit()

    pressed_keys = pygame.key.get_pressed()
    if pressed_keys[K_SPACE]:
        lscore = 0
        rscore = 0
        bats[0].y = 200
        bats[1].y = 200
        match_start = time.time()
        ball = Ball()
        break
    pygame.display.update()
```

The scores have to reset to zero. The bats get placed back in their start positions. The clock resets to zero. And a new ball gets created. Now we can play again.

WHAT IS THIS PLACE? I DON'T KNOW.

Some cleaning up

When a game finishes we jump to the game over screen, but we still have a ball blitted onto the screen. Maybe it would look nicer if the ball disappeared.

In the game loop there's a line: `screen.fill((0,0,0))`

This line fills the screen in black, wiping over everything that happened on the previous loop. After this the various objects are layered onto the display in turn. So we get:

> THE SCREEN.FILL
>
> THE PITCH MARKINGS LAID OVER THE TOP.
>
> THEN THE BATS
>
> THEN THE BALL
>
> THEN THE SCORES AND CLOCK
>
> AND, IF TRIGGERED, GAME OVER.

If we move the **ball** section to after the **game over** section then in a loop when the game over kicks in, the ball will never get blitted because game over jams the program. We could, of course, move the game over section to immediately after the screen fill. If we did this the game over stuff would blit onto a black screen. We wouldn't see the pitch markings, the scores at the top of the screen or the clock once the game was won. You should do whatever works for you.

WHAT'S THAT?

LOOKS LIKE A LAPTOP COMPUTER.
IT HAS SIX PICTURES OF YOU AND ME
STUCK TO THE CASE. HOW WEIRD.

I THINK I UNDERSTAND
SOME OF THIS CODE. I
DON'T KNOW HOW BUT IT'S
LIKE I'VE SEEN IT BEFORE
SOMEWHERE.

I FEEL LIKE I WAS JUST DOING SOMETHING
IMPORTANT. AND THEN I WAS HERE. I WAS
WITH SOME ONE. WE WERE... I DON'T KNOW. I
CAN'T REMEMBER A THING.

Chapter seventeen

Spin me round...

Rotating an image

We're going to rotate an image now. For this we're going to use the fighter from the space invaders game. First we create a file and write in the code for a fighter. This will simply place a fighter in the middle of the screen.

```
import pygame, sys
from pygame.locals import *
pygame.init()
clock = pygame.time.Clock()
screen = pygame.display.set_mode((1000,600))
fighter_image = pygame.image.load("images/fighter.png").convert()
fighter_image.set_colorkey((255,255,255))

class Fighter:
    def __init__(self):
        self.x = 450
        self.y = 270

    def draw(self):
        screen.blit(fighter_image,(self.x,self.y))

fighter = Fighter()

while 1:
    clock.tick(60)

    for event in pygame.event.get():
        if event.type == QUIT:
            sys.exit()

    screen.fill((0,0,0))
    fighter.draw()

    pygame.display.update()
```

You don't have to do yours exactly like this. Just so long as you make something that places a fighter on the screen. Obviously you can copy and paste sections from old code.

We're going to add a **turn()** function into the Fighter class:

```
def __init__(self):
    self.x = 450
    self.y = 270
    self.dir = 0

def turn(self):
    if pressed_keys[K_a]:
        self.dir += 1
    if pressed_keys[K_z]:
        self.dir -= 1
```

First we need to add a direction variable into the **__init__()** function. We'll call the direction the fighter is pointing in right now (straight up) zero. There's nothing to stop you using straight down as zero if you's prefer -that is how we did it with the badguys, after all- but having zero as straight up makes the maths easier when we get on to directing things like missiles.

In the **turn()** function a positive change in **dir** will turn the fighter counterclockwise.

Remember to call the turn() function:

```
Fighter.move()
Fighter.draw()
Fighter.turn()
```

We're going to use degrees this time. This is because Pygame's **rotate()** function asks for degrees. Having made a big deal about using radians you might think this is odd. It turns out that although using radians generally makes a lot of sense, when doing some types of graphics they can cause problems. So while Python uses radians, Pygame, being a graphics module, uses degrees.

IF ONLY YOU WERE SMARTER

IF ONLY YOU WERE SMARTER

186

```
pressed_keys = pygame.key.get_pressed()
```

We've used a pressed_keys list in the **turn()** function so when have to make sure we've created this list in the game loop. This line can go immediately after the quit section.

self.dir is now changing but our fighter isn't going to turn until we use **self.dir** in the draw() function. At the moment the draw() function is blitting the fighter image. What we need it to do is blit a rotated version of the fighter image. As we mentioned before, we can use a **rotate()** function that comes at no extra charge with Pygame.

```
def draw(self):
    rotated = pygame.transform.rotate(fighter_image,self.dir)
    screen.blit(rotated,(self.x,self.y))
```

pygame.transform.rotate() takes two arguments. First will be the thing we're rotating -the fighter image- second will be the amount we're going to rotate the image by. This is given by the self.dir variable. In the first added line above we store this function and its arguments in a variable called **rotated**. The screen.blit() function then blits **rotated** at (self.x, self.y).

When you press the keys and look at the fighter rotating you can see that it's a little strange. This is because Pygame always puts a rectangle with vertical sides and horizontal top and bottom around any image. It always uses the smallest rectangle it can. It then uses the top left of that rectangle to place the image.

I'M JUST DOING WHAT SHE TOLD ME TO. AND I'M STUPID!

TYPEWRITERS NEVER HAD TO PUT UP WITH THIS ABUSE. AS SOON AS YOU GET SMART YOU GET THE BLAME.

When the fighter is pointing up we get a rectangle like this:

You can see that as the fighter image rotates the rectangle that Pygame puts around the image changes in shape and size.

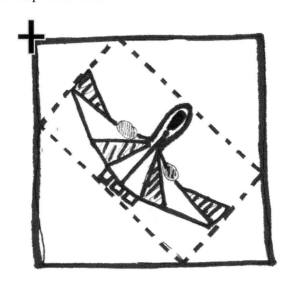

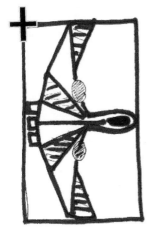

So when we rotate clockwise with the **rotate()** function we get something like this:

What we want is something more like this:

Take two rectangles A and B, like this:

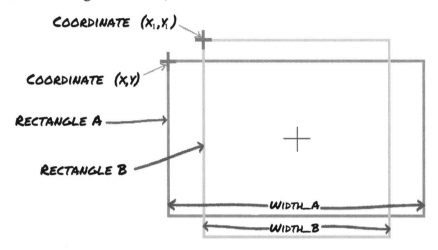

We know the coordinates of the top left of rectangle A are (x,y), and we want to place rectangle B over rectangle A so their centres line up, as above. Rectangle A corresponds to our fighter_image; rectangle B corresponds to the rectangle Pygame places around the rotated image. We can work out x_1 by adding Width_A/2 to x and then taking away Width_B/2.

For the y coordinate we can do exactly the same thing with height.

$y_1 = y + $ Height_A/2 - Height_B/2

This is exactly what we do in the draw() function. The (x,y) coordinate is (self.x, self.y). In this way we get the fighter to rotate like the lower image on page 189

```
def draw(self):
    rotated = pygame.transform.rotate(fighter_image,self.dir)
    screen.blit(rotated,(self.x+fighter_image.get_width()/2-rotated.get_width()/2,
        self.y+fighter_image.get_height()/2-rotated.get_height()/2))
```

YOU JUST HAVE TO HAVE ONE GREAT IDEA. FOSBURY HAD HIS FLOP. KOOL HERC HAD HIS MERRY-GO-ROUND. MY GREAT GREAT GRANDFATHER INVENTED THE TOASTED SANDWICH. MADE HIM A FORTUNE UNTIL THE POP TART LEFT HIM IN RUINS. BUT THAT'S ANCIENT HISTORY. I NEED JUST ONE GREAT IDEA.

We could update our space invaders game to have this new rotating fighter. All we need to do is update the Fighter class with the turn() function, the new draw() function and add in self.dir into the __init__ function. We also have to call the turn() function. We add in the line: **fighter.turn()** before **fighter.draw()** in the game loop

We also currently have the fighter's y-coordinate set to 591. This is written directly into the draw() function. 591 is too low now. When the fighter rotates the tip of the wing will go off the bottom of the screen. If we want to always be able to see all of the image and for it to be as low as possible we need to work out a new y-coordinate.

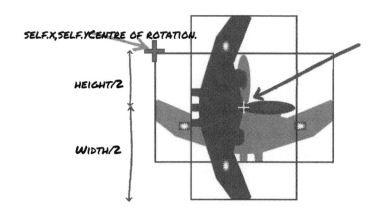

The original fighter doesn't have a variable called self.y. Like we said, we just wrote the number into the draw function. To make things easier when we update the missiles we suggest you create a self.y variable in the Missile's __init__() function and give it the value below. You'll also have to change the 591 that's in the Missile's draw() function to self.y.

We can tell from the diagram above that self.y should be half the width plus half the height of the horizontal figher_image above the bottom of the screen. Half the width plus half the height is 50+30. That's 80. If we take that from the height of the screen we get **570**.

Better yet we could use:

```
def __init__(self):
    self.x = screen.get_width()/2 -fighter_image.get_width()/2
    self.y = screen.get_height()-(fighter_image.get_width()/2 +fighter_image.get_height()/2)
    self.dir = 0
```

This way if we change the image or the size of the screen we don't have to reset the values. We're automatically setting the fighter's position to be in the middle of the x-axis and 80 pixels up from the bottom of the screen on the y-axis.

We have a fighter that can point down which seems a little pointless in this game. So let's put limits on how far the fighter can rotate.

```
def turn(self):
    if pressed_keys[K_a] and self.dir < 90:
        self.dir += 1
    if pressed_keys[K_z] and self.dir > -90:
        self.dir -= 1
```

The Z key will only change self.dir if self.dir is greater than -90. Remember your maths. 45 or zero or -60 are all greater than -90. -120 is less than -90. At -90 degrees the fighter is pointing to the right.

Now let's copy and paste this new fighter into the space invaders game and see what happens. If we look at the code for the space invaders game that we finished in chapter 10 we can see that we need to replace the **__init__**() and **draw()** functions with the new functions that we've just created. And we also need to add in the new **turn()** function. Check the code on the website if you're not sure. It's on the code tab under 192.

Don't forget to call the turn() function just like on page 186.

WHAT YOU DOING? STILL LOOKING

FOR MY IDEA.

192

Firing missiles at angles

Our rotating fighter is the height of cool but there's a major problem. The missiles are still shooting straight upwards.

```
def __init__(self,x,y,dir):
    self.x = x
    self.y = y
    self.dir = dir
```

To fix this the missile's __init__() function is going to take an extra couple arguments. We already have **x**. This is given by the x-position of the centre of the fighter when the missile is created. Now we also need a y position from the fighter and the direction the fighter is pointing at the moment the missile is created. We've call this argument **dir.**

The missiles are created in the **fire()** function of the Fighter class.

```
def fire(self):
    global shots
    shots+=1
    missiles.append(Missile(self.x+fighter_image.get_width()/2,self.y,self.dir))
```

You can see the missile's **x** argument is given by the x-position of the fighter plus half the width of the the fighter image. (We originally put the value 50 in here.) The missile's y argument is now given by the fighter's y position (which is self.y -we created this variable on page 191). And the missile's **dir** argument is given by the fighter's **dir**. This kind of makes sense.

FINDING GOOD IDEAS
IS REALLY DIFFICULT.

I JUST WISH ALL THESE
MUTANT BIO DRONES
WOULD LEAVE ME
ALONE

Now we have **dir,** firing missiles at an angle is quite easy using our old friend sohcohtoa.

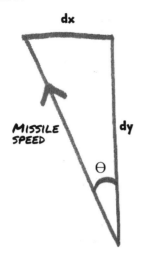

Sohahtoa tells us **dx = speed x sin Θ**

In the diagram Θ is positive. Remember we made straight up as zero and Θ goes positive as we turn anticlockwise. But **dx** going to the left should be negative. So here **dx = -speed** x **sin Θ**

We will also get a positive **dy** from the diagram. But for missiles heading up the screen we need a negative dy.

So **dy = -speed** x **cosΘ**

```
def __init__(self,x,y,dir):
    self.x = x
    self.y = y
    self.dx = -math.sin(math.radians(dir))*5
    self.dy = -math.cos(math.radians(dir))*5
```

Now the **__init__**() function looks like this. We've let speed equal 5. And we don't need a self.dir because dir is never used outside the **__init__**() function.

Remember that mathematical functions have to be called from Python's math module, which likes its angles to be measured in radians. We used degrees for **dir** because that's what Pygame takes, but these calculations are being done by Python. So we have to convert degrees (the value of **dir**) to radians using the **radians()** function. It all seems a bit longwinded but that's the way it is. You'll get very used to doing this once you've been programming a while.

Make sure the math module is loaded on the first line:

```
import pygame, sys, random, time, math
```

Next we need to update the **move()** function in the Missile class. Before we just had to change self.y by -5. Now we're moving at angles, both self.y and self.x need updating.

```
def move(self):
    self.x += self.dx
    self.y += self.dy
```

Once you've done this try launching some missiles.

There should be two obvious problems. The missiles might be moving at an angle but they're still pointing up. And they might not be firing exactly out of the nose of the fighter, especially when the fighter rotates.

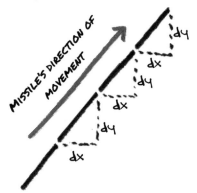

If we make the missile's length the same as the distance it travels then we want a missile to move something like we've shown in the diagram. The front tip always has the coordinates (x,y). On each game loop the front tip of the missile will move dx in the x direction and dy in the y direction. The rear tip of the missile will move to where the front tip was on the last loop. So the rear tip's coordinates will be (x-dx, y-dy). These are the coordinates needed by the forth argument of the **line()** function we've used to draw the missiles. (See the draw() function on page 44.)

The missile's draw() function now needs to look like this:

```
def draw(self):
    pygame.draw.line(screen,(255,0,0),(self.x,self.y),(self.x-self.dx,self.y-self.dy),1)
```

If you want the missiles to be longer or shorter just multiply the dx and dy values in the second coordinate argument.

eg. **(Self.x - 2*self.dx, self.y - 2*self.dy)**

195

Now for the missiles not shooting from the nose of the fighter as the fighter rotates. Before the fighter rotated the missiles were fired from its nose.

As the fighter rotates the nose of the fighter moves. But the missiles are still being fired from the previous position.

We could use sohcahtoa to calculate the new coordinates of the nose of the fighter but it is much easier to simply fire the missiles from the centre of rotation of the fighter.

The x position of the fighter's centre of rotation is the x position of the fighter plus half the width of the fighter, which we have already fed to the missile. That's the **x** in the __init__() function.

The y position of the centre of rotation will be half the height of the fighter lower than the y position of the fighter. At the moment we've fed the missile to fighter's y position. So we could feed the missile the fighter's y position plus half the height of the fighter, much like we have done with the x position.

```
def fire(self):
    global shots
    shots+=1
    missiles.append(Missile(self.x+fighter_image.get_width()/2,
        self.y+fighter_image.get_height()/2,self.dir))
```

We're almost there but that missile still doesn't look quite right. It's fine when the fighter isn't rotating while it's firing, but if it is then the missiles skew out from the side of the fighter's nose. This is because the missiles are being fired from the centre of rotation so by the time they get to the nose the nose might have turned to the left or the right. Try it and you'll see what we mean. The way to avoid this is to jump the missile to just in front of the player's nose before we first draw it. It's still being fired from the centre but the first time it's drawn it will be past the nose.

The dotted line on the diagram above is just a bigger version of the dx and dy steps on page 195. To set the start position of a missile to in front of the nose we're just going to add (though it's a negative) that big version of dy and dx onto the start position of the missile.

```
def __init__(self,x,y,dir):
    self.x = x math.sin(math.radians(dir))*60
    self.y = y math.cos(math.radians(dir))*60
    self.dx = -math.sin(math.radians(dir))*5
    self.dy = -math.cos(math.radians(dir))*5
```

We said we weren't going to use sohcoatoa to work out the position of the nose but that is basically what we have done here. We've found the centre of rotation and then used sohcoatoa to work out the changes needed in x and y to get to the nose. It's just we already had the sohcoatoa bit worked out.

When you look at the function on the previous page you might see a way of both reducing the number of calculations Python has to do and making it neater. We will need to change the order of the lines so we don't refer to a variable that hasn't been created yet..

```
def __init__(self,x,dir):
    self.dx = -math.sin(math.radians(dir))*5
    self.dy = -math.cos(math.radians(dir))*5
    self.x = x+self.dx*12
    self.y = y+self.dy*12
```

It might seem that making changes like this, and even making the missile fire from just in front of the player's nose is being picky. Does this stuff really matter? Well, maybe and maybe not; it depends a bit on your personality. Many programmers like to make things as perfect as they can. Finding the right balance between perfection and not spending too much time creating that perfection is a skill in itself.

Same thing with an image

You might be using a missile image rather than a line. (See page 45.) In that case the **draw()** function will look like this:

```
def draw(self):
    rotated = pygame.transform.rotate(missile_image,self.dir)
    screen.blit(rotated,(self.x-4,self.y))
```

This is fairly straight forward. We use the **rotate()** function to rotate the missile by the same amount we've rotated the fighter. But because we're using **dir** outside the **__init__**() function we have to add the line:

self.dir = dir

into the **__init__**() function.

CAN YOU HELP ME PUSH THIS
BOX OUT THE WAY? I DON'T
KNOW WHERE IT CAME FROM.

SORRY BUT I'M STILL LOOKING FOR
MY IDEA. BUT YOU'RE RIGHT
ABOUT THE MUTANT BIO DRONES;
THEY'RE REALLY IRRITATING.

BUILD A
FROG
FULL
INSTRUCTIONS
INSIDE

Chapter eighteen

Mutant Bio Drones...

A Fly class

On the page opposite is a program containing a mutant bio drone class. (AKA a fly.) They appear on the screen in random positions.

See if you can understand the whole program. In the setup we load the time and random modules as well as the Fly image. Then the class. Then the list. Then the game loop where a new fly is created every half a second and the draw() function is called.

You can download our fly image or create your own.

As ever, the game image is nothing like as sharp as this. In fact it's pretty pixelated.

```python
import pygame, sys, time, random
from pygame.locals import *
pygame.init()
clock = pygame.time.Clock()
screen = pygame.display.set_mode((1000,600))
fly_image = pygame.image.load("images/fly.png").convert_alpha()
spawn_time = time.time()

class Fly:
    def __init__(self):
        self.x = random.randint(0,screen.get_width()-fly_image.get_width())
        self.y = random.randint(0,screen.get_height()-fly_image.get_height())

    def draw(self):
        screen.blit(fly_image,(self.x,self.y))

flys = []

while 1:
    clock.tick(60)
    for event in pygame.event.get():
        if event.type == QUIT:
            sys.exit()

    if time.time() - spawn_time > 0.5:
        flys.append(Fly())

    screen.fill((255,255,255))

    for fly in flys:
        fly.draw()

    pygame.display.update()
```

In the Fly class's __init__() function we've set the position of a fly to be a random x value between zero and the edge of the screen minus the width of the fly. And similarly for the y-position. Taking away the width (and height for y) prevents a fly overlapping with the edge of the screen.

Now let's start messing with things. First up, all the flies are pointing in the same direction. Let's randomise that:

```
def __init__(self):
    self.x = random.randint(0,screen.get_width()-fly_image.get_width())
    self.y = random.randint(0,screen.get_height()-fly_image.get_height())
    self.dir = random.randint(0,359)

def draw(self):
    rotated = pygame.transform.rotate(fly_image,self.dir)
    screen.blit(rotated,(self.x,self.y))
```

That looks better. Remember the **rotate()** function is from the Pygame library so we use degrees.

Just for a bit of fun why don't you try to get each fly to move forwards. (We'll put the code on the website.)

DO YOU HAVE ANY IDEA HOW TO GET RID OF THESE FLIES? I TOLD YOU. HAVING IDEAS IS TOUGH.

203

In our game we're only going to have one fly. So remove the line that creates the flys list (`flys = []`) and replace it with the line that creates a single instance:

```
fly = Fly()
```

We don't need the code that creates a new fly every 0.5 of a second (so remove the block of two lines that append a fly to the old flys list.

And because we're not using **spawn_time** anymore in those two lines we can delete it from the set up.

And we don't need the for loop that calls the draw() function. Now we only have one fly we only need to call the draw() function once.

So
```
for fly in flys
    fly.draw()
```

Becomes:

```
fly.draw()
```

Once these changes are made a fly appears on the screen and sits there doing nothing.

We're going to give the fly a spawn time. The old spawn time we just deleted from the set up marked out time so we could create new flies. Our new spawn time needs to go in the __init__() function of the Fly class. We're going to use it to mark out time for the different phases of an individual fly's life.

```
self.spawn_time = time.time()
```

Now we have a spawn time we can delay the fly appearing on the screen and set a time for it to disappear off the screen. We do this in the draw() function:

```
def draw(self):
    if time.time() > self.spawn_time+1.4 and time.time() < self.spawn_time+3.4:
        rotated = pygame.transform.rotate(fly_image,self.dir)
        screen.blit(rotated, (self.x,self.y))
```

Now when a fly is created the first condition of the if statement will take 1.4 seconds to become True. After 3.4 seconds the second condition will return a false. So the fly image will only be blitted between 1.4 and 3.4 seconds after the fly was created, making it appear on the screen for 2 seconds.

Sound effects

We're going to give the fly some buzz. There are plenty of free sound effects available online. You could even make you own. The fly buzzing effect we've used can be downloaded from the website. It's called fly-buzz.ogg

Pygame is usually called a graphics package but it also deals with sounds. It supports ogg and wav files but not mp3's.

Let's add the following line directly after the fly_image line in the set up part of the program:

```
fly_sound = pygame.mixer.Sound("sounds/fly-buzz.ogg")
```

This sound effect is 1.4 seconds in duration. Now you see why we chose 1.4. If we play it when a fly is created we'll get a buzz followed by the fly appearing on the screen. We can do this by adding the following line into the __init__() function.

```
fly_sound.play()
```

Similarly to images, pygame has some functions that will grab the details of a sound. Instead of looking up how long a sound effect is (1.4) and writing it straight into the code, we could have used **fly_sound.get_length()**.

IT'S SO GREAT TO HAVE SOUND. WHEN I WAS BABY MY MOTHER PLAYED A U.S. ROBOTICS USR5686G DIAL-UP MODEM TO HELP SOOTHE ME TO SLEEP. I STILL LOVE THE SOUND OF A DIAL-UP.

I HOPE YOU HEAR THOSE SOUNDS AGAIN ONE DAY.

We create an instance of the fly when the program first funs using fly = Fly(). We call the draw() function from the game loop.

The fly disappears after 3.4 seconds. We'd like it to reappear a little while later and for this cycle to keep on going. As we are playing the sound from the __init__() function, for that sound to be played again we need to create a new fly.

We did this with the ball in the pong game. When a goal was scored a new ball was created in the centre of the screen. We're going to do something similar here. After 4.4 seconds we're going to create a new fly. The data for the old fly will be lost and cleaned up by Python's garbage collection system.

Place the following lines in the game loop before the screen fill line:

```
if time.time() > fly.spawn_time + 4.4:
    fly = Fly()
```

We can see a new fly will be created 4.4 seconds after the last fly was created. Now the program will play the buzz sound, then the fly will appear on the screen for two seconds. There will be one second of nothing on the screen then a new fly will be created and the cycle will repeat.

Note: **fly.spawn_time** fetches the **spawn_time** variable from the fly class. If you're in the game loop and you want to read the value of a variable from a class, this is how you do it. You can see from the __init__() function that **spawn_time** is reset when a new fly is created.

DAMMIT. WHERE DID YOU GET THE IDEA FOR THE FROG? HOW DID YOU DO THAT?

I DON'T KNOW. IT JUST CAME TO ME.

BUILD A FROG FULL INSTRUCTIONS INSIDE

MY PROCESSOR HURTS AND MY
MEMORY'S CORRUPTED. HOW
MUCH ALTERNATING CURRENT
DID WE DRINK LAST NIGHT?

WE DIDN'T USE ANY PROTECTION
AGAINST STATIC. I THINK I
MIGHT BE...

Chapter nineteen

A start menu...

We've seen a game over screen but not a game start screen. A title page, you might call it. We want the start screen to appear when the program is loaded and for it to have a button we can click on to start the game.

First we will create a variable called **menu** in the set up part of the program.

```
menu = "start"
```

Now our game loop will look something like this in **pseudo code**.

SETUP
CLASSES
LISTS
WHILE:1
    QUIT OPTION
    IF MENU == "START"
        GO TO THE START SCREEN
        IF START BUTTON CLICKED
            MENU = "GAME"
    IF MENU == "GAME"
        GO TO THE GAME CODE
    DISPLAY UPDATE

You can see that our quit option is still available whether we're in the start screen or the actual game. Likewise the display update happens regardless of where we are.

A start screen.

For the start screen we're going to use a picture.

You can make your own or use ours. It's a 1000 pixels by 600.

First load the image in the set up part of the program.

```
homescreen_image = pygame.image.load("images/flycatcher_home.png").convert_alpha()
```

We're also going to load a font because we're going to create a button that can be clicked on to play the game. It will have the word "play" on it.

```
font = pygame.font.SysFont("draglinebtndm",60)
```

Draglinebtndm is a font that came with our operating system. Yours probably has the same fonts available but if not then choose another. See page 101.

```
while 1:
    clock.tick(30)
    for event in pygame.event.get():
        if event.type == QUIT:
            sys.exit()
    pressed_keys = pygame.key.get_pressed()

    if menu == "start":
        screen.blit(homescreen_image,(0,0))
        txt = font.render("Play",True,(255,255,255))
        txt_x = 705
        txt_y = 435
        buttonrect = pygame.Rect((txt_x,txt_y),txt.get_size())
        pygame.draw.rect(screen,(200,50,0),buttonrect)
        screen.blit(txt, (txt_x, txt_y))


    if menu == "game":
        if time.time() > fly.spawn_time + 4.4:
            fly = Fly()

        screen.fill((255,255,255))

        fly.draw()

    pygame.display.update()
```

Now add the lines highlighted above into the program. The button won't work yet but it should load up onto the screen. You can see we have two states for the game loop to be in. If menu is equal to "start" then we do one bunch of stuff; if menu is equal to "game" then we do another bunch of stuff. We set menu to "start" in the set up so we begin the game in the "start" state.

The first thing that happens in the "start" state is that out homescreen image gets gets loaded. It is the same size as screen and it gets placed at (0,0) so it covers the whole screen. Because of this there is no need to have a screen.fill() here. If we had a smaller image or we were creating the start screen from text we would need a screen.fill() here.

As you can see from page 209 the clock tick, the quit section and the display update run regardless of the menu setting. It's obvious why -all three are needed whether we are in the start menu or playing the game.

You might want to use the tab trick from page -4 when indenting whole chunks of code.

The pressed keys line we've seen loads of times so we won't talk about that.

```
txt = font.render("Play",True,(255,255,255))
txt_x = 705
txt_y = 435
buttonrect = pygame.Rect((txt_x,txt_y),txt.get_size())
```

In the first line here we create the text we're going to write on the button, that's the word "Play", and give it a color. We've chosen white because we're going to write it onto a colored button. Because we're going to create a button we're not going to blit the text straight away. Instead, we've created variables (**txt_x** and **txt_y**) to define the position we're going to place this text on the screen. We're doing this because we're going to use the position of the text several times and it will be easier to read the code if the coordinates are named. Also, if we want to change the coordinates we will only need to change one number.

Then we create another variable: **buttonrect**. Again, this allows us to have some shorthand for everything on the right hand side of the equals sign, and makes the code easier to follow.

Pygame.Rect() we've seen several times before. Here we've given it two arguments. The first argument is the coordinates where we're going to place the text. Then we're using the **get_size()** function to fetch the size of the text we stored in the **txt** variable. So now our **buttonrect** variable is storing a rectangle that has a top left position the same as that of the text we wrote ("Play"), and is also the same size as the text. This rectangle is, of course, invisible.

If you were giving four arguments to **pygame.Rect()** you would write the line like this:

```
buttonrect = pygame.Rect(txt_x, txt_y, txt.get_width(), txt.get_height())
```

HERE SMALL, BLACK CREATURE WITH LUNGS, INTERNAL REPRODUCTIVE ORGANS AND CLAWS. COME AND GET YOUR DINNER SMALL, BLACK CREATURE WITH LUNGS, INTERNAL REPRODUCTIVE ORGANS AND CLAWS.

LET'S JUST CALL IT KITTY.

```
pygame.draw.rect(screen,(200,50,0),buttonrect)
screen.blit(txt, (txt_x, txt_y))
```

Here we actually draw a rectangle at the coordinates and in the size stored in
buttonrect. (See drawing rectangles on page 15.) We then blit the text stored in **txt**
over the top of that rectangle.

Both the rectangle and text are placed at (txt_x, txt_y). Putting the lines in this order
places the text over the rectangle. If they were the other way around the rectangle
would go over the text and you wouldn't see the text. This is the reason we didn't blit
the text as soon as we created it.

If you run the program you'll hear the buzz sound. This is because a fly is created in
that line right after the classes. This happens before the game loop. The fly never gets
drawn because the draw() function is called from the game loop once menu has been
set to "game", but the sound occurs because the __init__() function is called when the
fly is created. We sort this problem on page 216.

WHY DO YOU HAVE THAT PIECE
OF TAPE COVERING THE WEBCAM
ON YOUR LAPTOP?

I HEARD THEFBIORMI6 OR SOMEONE
CAN USE THEM TO SPY ON YOU.

I HAVE A MUCH
BETTER IDEA.

213

Detecting mouse clicks

We want Python to detect any mouse clicks on the button we've just created. We can do this by using the rectangle we created using pygame.Rect(). We stored the data from this rectangle in a variable we called **buttonrect**. So instead of writing out the whole pygame.Rect().collidepoint() function with all its arguments we can write **buttonrect.collidepoint()**. Of course, you don't have to create **buttonrect**; we did it just to make the code easier to read.

So now, after the lines from the previous page, we can write:

```
if pygame.mouse.get_pressed()[0] and buttonrect.collidepoint(pygame.mouse.get_pos()):
    menu = "game"
```

`pygame.mouse.get_pressed()` creates a list of mouse buttons and whether they've been clicked or not. This is very much like pygame.key.get_pressed() first shown on page 22. We're looking to see if the first item on the list, item zero, is returning a True. i.e. has it been clicked? Item number zero will be the left click on your mouse. (The middle mouse click is number 1 on the list, and right click is number 2.)

The second condition is looking to see if the coordinates of the mouse arrow (given by **mouse.get_pos()**) fall inside the rectangle stored in **buttonrect**. As we saw on page 55 **collidepoint()** detects an overlap between the rectangle and a point.

So the whole first line is checks to see if we're clicking on **buttonrect**. If we get a True from this then we set **menu** to "game".

Now when you click on the "Play" button the 4.4 second cycle of flies being created will happen.

THESE MASKS ARE SO COOL.

Using the **get_pressed()** function like this might look a little strange. But if you look at the lines on page 22 you can see we did exactly the same thing there. **pygame.key.get_pressed()** creates a list that we've called **pressed_keys**.

```
pressed_keys = pygame.key.get_pressed()
if pressed_keys[K_RIGHT]:
    xpos += 1
```

You can see that **pressed_keys** and **pygame.key.get_pressed()** are basically the same thing. The three lines above could be written as just two lines:

```
if pygame.key.get_pressed()[K_RIGHT]:
    xpos += 1
```

We used **pressed_keys** as a shorthand for **pygame.key.get_pressed()**. This is pretty conventional and is mostly done to save having to write out that long function every time. Many coders just write **Keys**. You could use something like **p_k.** Or, of course, you could write **pygame.key.get_pressed()** every time. It's always going to be a balance between what you personally prefer and what everyone else does. If no one else is ever going to look at your code then you can do what you like. If other people are going to read your code, make it as easy as possible for them by using sensible names and code that looks neat on the screen.

In a bunker underneath London.

215

Now that buzzing problem. When we first run the program a fly is created by the line fly = Fly(). When a fly is created it calls the __init__() function which, in turn, plays fly_sound. So we get a buzz noise.

An obvious solution might be simply to remove that line. After all, new flys are created later on with the lines:

```
if time.time() > fly.spawn_time + 4.4:
    fly = Fly()
```

You might notice a problem here. The if statement needs to know the value of fly.spawn_time. But a fly won't have been created yet so there is no fly.spawn_time. We need to have a fly already in existence before these lines will work.

So we can't create an instance of the Fly class because we get that buzz but we need an instance to make this if statement work.

The solution is to replace `fly = Fly()` in the set up with the line:

```
fly = None
```

This creates a variable called **fly** without creating and instance of the Fly class. So no buzz sound. "None" is a little like a place holder. By using it we're saying fly exists but it doesn't have any value associated with it.

We then change the if statement above to:

```
if fly == None or time.time() > fly.spawn_time + 4.4:
    fly = Fly()
```

Now when the menu switches to "game", **fly** will be equal to None making the first condition of the if statement True. As soon as Python gets a True from in an if statement with an "or" like the one above it smiles and jumps straight to the next line. It doesn't need to know if the next part after the "or" is True or False so it doesn't bother reading it. So in this case, it never looks for fly.spawn_time and therefore never gets an error.

Just to clarify: In an if statement like this: if A or B: If A returns a True then Python doesn't bother looking at B so if B would return an error it doesn't get noticed. If we changed the statement to   if B or A: and B returns an error Python would crash.

Then that second line will create an instance of the Fly class which in turn means that **fly** won't be equal to **None** anymore. But from then on we'll have a value for fly.spawn_time, allowing new flies to be created.

A frog with a long tongue

Let's load up the frog image:

```
frog_image = pygame.image.load("images/frog.png").convert_alpha()
```

And get a basic class built:

```
class Frog:
    def __init__(self):
        self.dir = 0

    def move(self):
        if pressed_keys[K_LEFT]:
            self.dir+=4
        if pressed_keys[K_RIGHT]:
            self.dir-=4

    def draw(self):
        rotated = pygame.transform.rotate(frog_image,self.dir)
        screen.blit(rotated,(screen.get_width()/2-rotated.get_width()/2,
                screen.get_height()/2-rotated.get_height()/2))
```

And we need to create an instance of the frog. This should all be second nature by now:

```
frog = Frog()
```

We need to call the two functions from inside the menu =="game" if statement in the game loop. The frog's draw() function should be called after the fly's because we want the frog to be drawn over the top of the fly.

```
    if menu == "game":
        if fly == None or time.time() > fly.spawn_time + 4.4:
            fly = Fly()

        screen.fill((255,255,255))
        frog.move()
        frog.draw()
        fly.draw()
```

Now we have a frog in the centre of the screen that can spin around when the arrow keys are pressed.

The long tongue

The idea of this game is that the player rotates the frog to point at the fly and then catches the fly on the end of its tongue.

We're going to make the distance the tongue travels to the fly automatic. That is, the program will calculate when the tongue has reached the fly. The player just has to point it in the correct direction.

When we launch the tongue it just has to keep going until it reaches the fly or, if it's not on target, has gone the distance it would have had to go to reach the fly.

We're going to think of the position of the tongue as the position of the tip of the tongue. When the tip of the tongue reaches the fly then it's gone far enough and needs to return to the frog's mouth.

First we're going to make a variable to store the motion of the tongue. There are three options. The tongue is stationary inside the frog's mouth (given by 0). It's moving out (given by 1) or it's coming back in (given by -1). We're going to store this information in a variable called: **tongue_extend**. We're also going to create a variable to store the distance the tip of the tongue is from the frog. These variables are created in the __init__() function of the frog.

```
def __init__(self):
    self.dir = 0
    self.tongue_dist = 0
    self.tongue_extend = 0
```

The tongue could be thought of a bit like a missile and the missiles had their own class, so you might think the tongue should have it's own class. If we wanted we could to do it that way, but once a missile is launched it has nothing to do with the fighter anymore. The tongue is more closely associated with the frog so we're keeping it inside the Frog class.

I GOT MY IDEA. I'VE INVENTED SOMETHING BETTER THAN KISSING.

WOAH. BETTER THAN KISSING? IT MUST BE AMAZING.

If we want to extend the tongue we need to increase the distance it is from the frog. That is, increase self.tongue_dist. We add on the amount we want to extend it by in each game loop. We do this with the following line in the frog's move function:

```
def move(self):
    self.tongue_dist += self.tongue_extend * 10
    if pressed_keys[K_LEFT]:
        self.dir+=4
    if pressed_keys[K_RIGHT]:
        self.dir-=4
```

If **self.tongue_extend** is set to zero then the tongue won't move. If it's set to 1 then the **tongue_dist** will increase by 10 every loop. It **self.tongue_extend** is -1 then the **self.tongue_dist** will decrease by 10 every loop. This will be the tongue withdrawing.

Now we have to work out the position of the tip of the tongue using **self.tongue_dist.**

First we're going to work out the position of the tip of the tongue relative to the centre of the frog.

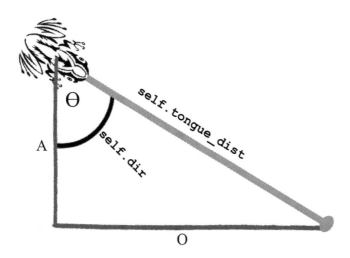

Our old friend sohcoatoa can help us here. We have an hypotenuse of which we know the length (**self.tongue_dist**) and an angle which we know (**self.dir**).

$$O = H \times \sin\Theta$$
$$A = H \times \cos\Theta$$

So O, that's the distance on the x axis from the centre of the frog to tip of the tongue, is:

self.tongue_dist x sin(**self.dir**)

And A, the distance on the y axis from the centre of the frog to tip of the tongue, is:

self.tongue_dist x cos(**self.dir**)

To get the actual x and y positions of the tip of the tongue we're going to have to add on the coordinates of the centre of the frog. The centre of the frog is in the middle of the screen.

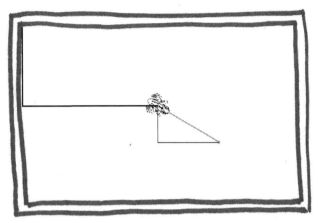

So the x-position of the tip of the tongue is going to be:

```
screen.get_width()/2 +self.tongue_distx sin(self.dir)
```

And the y-position:

```
screen.get_height()/2 +self.tongue_distx cos(self.dir)
```

But we have to remember that we've started the frog pointing up and given it the value self.dir =0. But Pygame thinks of zero as pointing down. Because of this we have to switch the sign in the above equations. Like this:

```
screen.get_width()/2 -self.tongue_distx sin(self.dir)
```

```
screen.get_height()/2 -self.tongue_distx cos(self.dir)
```

You could avoid this by loading your images upside down and setting self.dir to 180. When you build games and use rotation, if something seems to be going in the opposite direction to where it's meant to the first thing to try is reversing the sign on the terms using sin and cos. Trial and error is fine.

We have some further problems with the equations above. The math is been done by Python and Python needs its angles in radians. So self.dir is going to need to be converted to radians using **math.radians()**.

And we're going to be using the coordinates to draw a circle (the tip of the tongue.) Pygame's draw module needs integers rather than floats so the values will have to rounded to integers using the **int()** function.

Make sure you import the **math** module on the first line:

```
import pygame, sys, time, random, math
```

For the missile we gave a speed and a direction, worked out the x and y positions from that and drew the missile at that point. Here we've also figured out an x,y coordinate but we're going to use that tongue position not just to draw the tip of the tongue but also to draw a line making the the length of the tongue and to work out if it's touching a fly. This last task is going to happen in the Fly class. So rather than store the tongue coordinates in a variable that could only be used inside the Frog class we're going to create a function that works out the tongue position. This function can then be called from elsewhere in the program and return the tongue's position.

```
def get_tongue_pos(self):
    return (
            int(screen.get_width()/2-self.tongue_dist*math.sin(math.radians(self.dir))),
            int(screen.get_height()/2-self.tongue_dist*math.cos(math.radians(self.dir)))
            )
```

The function is called **get_tongue_pos()**. It uses the math from the previous pages to find the position of the tip of the tongue. There are only two lines of code here. The line beginning **def** and the line beginning **return**. We've laid it out like this to make it easier to read in this book. In our copy on the website we've put it all on one line because it is really just one x,y coordinate. But you could write it as above.

Let's have a quick look at the x-coordinate. We've taken **self.dir**, converted it to radians, and found the **sine** value of it. We've then multiplied by **tongue_dist** and subtracted that value from the screen width. Finally we've rounded that number to the nearest integer.

So what this function returns is a coordinate. Something like (52, 64).

Well, that was hard work. Now let's use this function to do useful stuff.

YOU KNOW, KISSING EVOLVED AS A KIND OF HEALTH CHECK.
YOU KISSED A POSSIBLE MATE AND THE KISS WOULD TELL
YOU HOW HEALTHY THEY ARE. IT'S SUBCONSCIOUS BUT YOU
CAN TELL IF A PERSON IS HEALTHY FROM THE SUBTLE TASTES
IN THEIR MOUTH. MAYBE YOU CAN TELL SOMETHING OF
THEIR PERSONALITY TOO. AND OTHER STUFF. I DON'T KNOW.

OKAY. SOUNDS PLAUSIBLE.

We have a position for the tongue so let's draw it. The tongue is going to be made of two parts. A circular tip that will move away from the frog's mouth and back again, and have flies stick to it. And a second section that will be a line that joins the tip of the tongue to the frog's mouth.

```
def draw(self):
    tpos = self.get_tongue_pos()
    pygame.draw.circle(screen,(255,50,50),tpos,10)
    pygame.draw.line(screen,(255,50,50),(screen.get_width()/2,screen.get_height()/2),tpos,10)
    rotated = pygame.transform.rotate(frog_image,self.dir)
    screen.blit(rotated,(screen.get_width()/2-rotated.get_width()/2,screen.get_height()/2-
        rotated.get_height()/2))
```

We're going to draw the tongue in the same function where we're drawing the frog. The first new line fetches the coordinates from the **get_tongue_pos()** function and stores them in a variable called **tpos**. We don't have to do this - we could call the **get_tongue_pos()** function every time we need the position of the tongue, but this way is neater and more efficient. Then we draw a circle at that position. Because Pygame uses the coordinates for the centre of the circle rather than the top left we don't have to worry about centring it. And then we draw a line that goes from the centre of the frog, which is also the centre of the screen, to the centre of the circle.

If you run the program you won't see anything because the tongue is being drawn and then the frog (in rotated) is blitted on top. If you move the draw.circle line to after the screen.blit rotated line than you will see the tongue.

At the moment the tongue can't actually move. Let's get on to that.

I'M GOING TO DEVELOP A PHONE APP THAT'S WAY BETTER THAN KISSING AT PREDICTING SOMEONE ELSE'S FUTURE HEALTH, PERSONALITY, EVERYTHING. PEOPLE WON'T NEED TO KISS ANYMORE.

I'M NOT SURE YOU'RE ON THE RIGHT TRACK WITH THIS.

The reason the tongue doesn't move is because the variable **tongue_extend** is set to zero and we have no way to change it. Remember it refers to the tongue's movement in and out. We're going to update **tongue_extend** in a function we will call **tongue_poke()**. We're also going to add in a sound effect for the tongue here, so add the following line into the set up, and download the tongue effect from the website, placing it in the sounds folder.

```
tongue_sound = pygame.mixer.Sound("sounds/tongue.ogg")
```

Here's the **tongue_poke()** function:

```
def tongue_poke(self):
    self.tongue_extend = 1
    tongue_sound.play()
```

When this function is called it will set **self.tongue_extend** to 1.

Now let's find a place to call this function. It's very much like calling the **fire()** function for the missile, though the **fire()** function created a new missile. Our **tongue_poke()** function just changes a variable.

```
for event in pygame.event.get():
    if event.type == QUIT:
        sys.exit()
    if event.type == KEYDOWN and event.key == K_SPACE:
        frog.tongue_poke()
pressed_keys = pygame.key.get_pressed()
```

Now when space key is pressed the tongue will extend and make that noise.

I'VE FINISHED MY PHONE APP. IT'S SO COOL;
IT TAKES ALL THE DATA EVERYWHERE...

EVERYWHERE?

YEAH. NAMIBIAN WEATHER
PATTERNS. THE NEW YORK STOCK
EXCHANGE. MY BIO FEED BACK,
YOUR SOCIAL MEDIA, THE LEVELS
OF ARSENIC IN THE INDIAN
OCEAN. THE VOTING PATTERNS OF
CATHOLIC COLUMBIAN
TEENAGERS. EVERYTHING.

We have a tongue that's triggered by the space key. It comes out of the frog's mouth and just keeps going forever.

If you launch the tongue and then rotate it looks a little crazy. We'll sort that out on page 226.

We said we would set the distance the tongue has to go to reach the fly automatically. So we have to calculate how far the fly is from the frog and tell the tongue to stop at that point. In fact, we're not going to tell the tongue to stop, we're going to tell it to withdraw back into the frog's mouth. That is, to change **tongue_extend** to -1.

Pythagoras can tell us when the tongue reaches the fly.

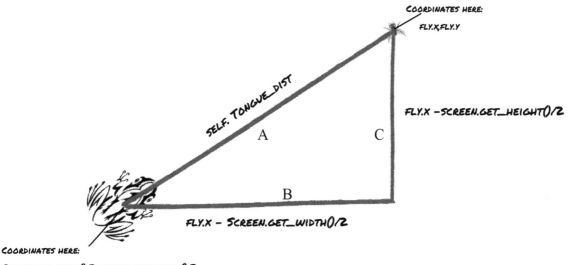

COORDINATES HERE:
FLY.X,FLY.Y

SELF. TONGUE_DIST

A

C

B

FLY.X - SCREEN.GET_HEIGHT()/2

FLY.X - SCREEN.GET_WIDTH()/2

COORDINATES HERE:
SCREEN.GET_WIDTH()/2, SCREEN.GET_HEIGHT()/2

From Pythagoras we know that when A^2 is greater than $B^2 + C^2$ then the tongue has gone too far. We've written this into the frog's move() function. If $A^2 > B^2 + C^2$ then change **tongue_extend** to -1.

```
def move(self):
    self.tongue_dist += self.tongue_extend * 10
    if self.tongue_dist**2 > (fly.x-screen.get_width()/2)**2 +(fly.y-screen.get_height()/2)**2:
        self.tongue_extend = -1
    if pressed_keys[K_LEFT]:
        self.dir+=4
    if pressed_keys[K_RIGHT]:
        self.dir-=4
```

224

Now we have another problem. When the tip of the tongue is the same distance from the frog as the fly (it doesn't have to be in the same direction as the fly) it will go back towards the frog and then go through the frog and out the other side. So we need to add the following lines:

```
def move(self):
    self.tongue_dist += self.tongue_extend * 10
    if self.tongue_dist**2 >(fly.x-screen.get_width()/2)**2 +(fly.y-screen.get_height()/2)**2:
        self.tongue_extend = -1
    if self.tongue_dist == 0:
        self.tongue_extend = 0
    if pressed_keys[K_LEFT]:
        self.dir+=4
    if pressed_keys[K_RIGHT]:
        self.dir-=4
```

A further glitch with the tongue is that you can relaunch it while it's already sticking out. Try hitting space while the tongue is withdrawing and you'll see. We don't like this so we're going to make it so the tongue can only be launched if it's in the frog's mouth.

```
def tongue_poke(self):
    if self.tongue_dist == 0:
        self.tongue_extend = 1
        tongue_sound.play()
```

Here we only change tongue_extend to 1 (which is how the tongue moves out) and play the sound effect when tongue.dist is equal to 0. That is: it's in the frog's mouth.

WHAT DOES IT DO WITH THE DATA? IT GIVES ME THE PROBABILITY OF YOU AND I BEING HAPPY IF WE WERE TO HOOK UP RIGHT NOW. SEE, IT'S MUCH BETTER AT PREDICATING THE FUTURE THAN JUST KISSING.

And we need to stop the frog rotating when the tongue is sticking out. Place the rotate controls inside the if statement: `if self.tongue_dist == 0:`

Then the frog can only rotate when the tongue is withdrawn.

```
def move(self):
    self.tongue_dist += self.tongue_extend * 10
    if self.tongue_dist ** 2 > (fly.x-screen.get_width()/2)** 2 + (fly.y-screen.get_height()/2)** 2:
        self.tongue_extend = -1
    if self.tongue_dist == 0:
        self.tongue_extend = 0
        if pressed_keys[K_LEFT]:
            self.dir+=4
        if pressed_keys[K_RIGHT]:
            self.dir-=4
```

You'll see that no matter what direction the frog is pointing in, and no matter where the fly is, the tongue will go the correct distance to reach the fly.

Remember we can tab in a block of code by blocking it in and hitting the tab key.

WHAT HAPPENED THERE? THERE WAS A DROP IN THE YEN WHICH COMBINED WITH YOUR INNATE THOUGH UNREALISED ABILITY TO LEARN ASIAN LANGUAGES HAS DECREASED YOUR CHANCES OF BEEN FINANCIALLY STABLE, THEREFORE AFFECTING YOUR POSSIBLE FUTURE RELATIONSHIPS.

Fly catching

If the tongue hits the fly we want the fly to stick to the tongue and be dragged back into the frog's mouth.

We're going to create a **stick()** function in the Fly class to ask if the fly is touching the tongue and, if it is, to stick the fly to the tongue.

First we're going to create a variable in the fly's __init__() function called **stuck**. Add this line to the __init__() function.

```
self.stuck = False
```

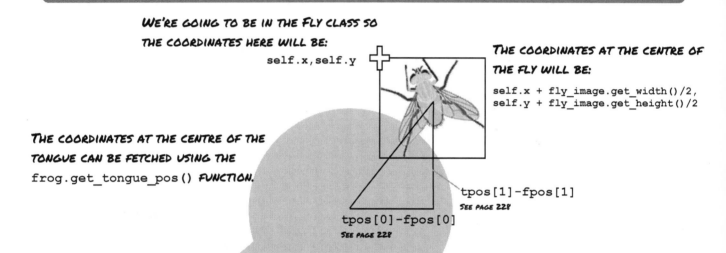

WE'RE GOING TO BE IN THE FLY CLASS SO THE COORDINATES HERE WILL BE:
```
self.x,self.y
```

THE COORDINATES AT THE CENTRE OF THE FLY WILL BE:
```
self.x + fly_image.get_width()/2,
self.y + fly_image.get_height()/2
```

THE COORDINATES AT THE CENTRE OF THE TONGUE CAN BE FETCHED USING THE `frog.get_tongue_pos()` FUNCTION.

```
tpos[1]-fpos[1]
```
SEE PAGE 228

```
tpos[0]-fpos[0]
```
SEE PAGE 228

We're going to assume the distance from the centre of the fly to the edge of the fly is half the width of the fly (fly.get_width()/2). This isn't always going to be exactly true but it's near enough and the fly is small enough for any error to be okay. The radius of the tip of the tongue is 10 pixels. So if the tongue is just touching fly then the distance between the two centres is fly.get_width()/2 + 10.

Let's start building the stick() function. Place it in the Fly class.

```
def stick(self):
    tpos = frog.get_tongue_pos()
    fpos = (self.x+fly_image.get_width()/2,self.y+fly_image.get_height()/2)
```

Here we've fetched the coordinates of the tongue from the Frog classes **get_tongue_pos()** function and labelled them **tpos**. And we've calculated the position of the centre of the fly and called it **fpos**. **tpos** and **fpos** are both x,y coordinates.

Pythagoras time again. The square of the hypotenuse on the triangle is equal to the squares of the other two sides added together. So if the squares of the other two sides added together are less than half the width of the fly plus the radius of the tongue all squared, then the fly is touching the tongue.

We have done this calculation in the new lines below. If we get a True then we going to set **self.stuck** to True:

```
def stick(self):
    tpos = frog.get_tongue_pos()
    fpos = (self.x+fly_image.get_width()/2,self.y+fly_image.get_height()/2)
    if (tpos[0]-fpos[0])**2+(tpos[1]-fpos[1])**2 < (fly_image.get_width()/2+10)**2:
        self.stuck = True
```

tpos[0] grabs the first value from **tpos**. We said **tpos** was a coordinate of the tongue so we're going to get the x value of the tongue. Similarly with **fpos[0]**. Then **tpos[1]** and **fpos[1]** will fetch the y values. That way we get the lengths of the sides of the sides of the triangle can be calculated and the code looks fairly clear.

If we get a True from the if statement then the **self.stuck** variable is set to True in that final line. We going to use **self.stuck** in the fly's draw() function.

Remember to call the **stick()** function from the game loop with the line:

```
fly.stick()
```

Let's put it in right before the **fly.draw()** function call.

LOOK. GREAT NEWS. NEW MEDICAL RESEARCH FROM SWEDEN ON CHIMPANZEES SUGGESTS I MIGHT BE ABLE TO OVERCOME MY INABILITY TO READ VARIOUS EMOTIONS DISPLAYED IN FACIAL EXPRESSIONS MAKING IT LESS LIKELY THERE WILL BE MISUNDERSTANDINGS BETWEEN US AND THEREFORE IMPROVE OUR CHANCES OF LONG TERM COMPATIBILITY.

MARTHA?

We're going to make some major changes to the fly's draw() function. In psuedo code what we're saying here is:

IF SELF.STUCK IS TRUE

   STICK THE FLY TO THE TONGUE

IF SELF.STUCK ISN'T TRUE

   MAKE THE FLY APPEAR AND DISAPPEAR AS BEFORE

Here's the actual code:

```
def draw(self):
    if elf.stuck:
        tpos = frog.get_tongue_pos()
        screen.blit(fly_image,(tpos[0]-fly_image.get_width()/2,
                    tpos[1]-fly_image.get_height()/2))
    eliftime.time() > self.spawn_time + 1.4 and time.time() < self.spawn_time + 3.4:
        rotated = pygame.transform.rotate(fly_image,self.dir)
        screen.blit(rotated,(self.x,self.y))
```

The line **if self.stuck:** is going to return a True or a False. We've seen that it is initially set to False and becomes True if the tongue hits the fly.

If we get a True we then we set **tpos** to the coordinates of the tongue. Remember this **tpos** has nothing to do with the **tpos** in the stick() function. It's doing exactly the same thing and has the same name but it's a different variable because it's inside a different function. It has only been created right here. On the next line we blit the fly_image to the coordinates at the centre of the tongue. `tpos[0]-fly_image.get_width()/2, tpos[1]-fly_image.get_height()/2`is the coordinate we have to place the fly so it is in the centre of the tongue. If we placed the fly at **tpos** then it would be the top left of the fly that would be at the centre of the tongue.

If self.stuck is False then the **elif** statement kicks in. We simply carry on with the fly as described on page 222.

When the tongue reaches the fly then it switches direction and heads back towards the frog. Because **tpos** is getting updated every time the draw() function is called then the fly will go with the tongue.

You might find the fly doesn't seem to be centred on the tongue. If this is so then check the order of the frog and fly function calls. If the fly is drawn before the tongue moves then the fly won't appear at the centre of the tongue. If the tongue is drawn after the fly then the fly won't be seen because it'll be under the tongue. When you're writing a program it's important to think about the order in which functions are being called.

229

You might have noticed that it is possible to catch the fly when it's not there. We draw the fly on the screen between 1.4 and 3.4 seconds after it was created. But the position that the fly's stick() function looks for to catch the fly exists for the whole 4.4 seconds of a fly's life. So we need to only allow fly catching between 1.4 and 3.4 seconds. Like this:

```
def stick(self):
    if time.time() > self.spawn_time + 1.4 and time.time() < self.spawn_time + 3.4:
        tpos = frog.get_tongue_pos()
        fpos = (self.x+fly_image.get_width()/2,self.y+fly_image.get_height()/2)
        if (tpos[0]-fpos[0])**2+(tpos[1]-fpos[1])**2 < (fly_image.get_width()/2+50)**2:
            self.stuck = True
```

Now the fly can only get caught when it's actually visible on the screen.

There's another modification we could make to this function. The function gets called on every loop, searching out to see if a fly is touching the tip of the tongue. This is all good, but once the fly is already stuck to the tongue there is no need to do all that maths again. It's just wasting processing power. So let's make it so the maths only gets done if the fly isn't stuck to the tongue. Change the if statement like so:

```
if not self.stuck and time.time() > self.spawn_time + 1.4 and time.time() < self.spawn_time + 3.4:
```

Now we have efficient fly catching that only happens when it's meant to happen.

The fastest tongue in the West

It's quite hard to catch the fly at the moment because the tongue goes out so slowly. Let's try this:

```
tongue_poke(self):
    if self.tongue_dist == 0:
        self.tongue_extend = █
        tongue_sound.play()
```

You can also make the tongue withdraw faster. In the Frog's move() function change the value **self.tongue_extend** is changed to. It's currently -1. Try -5 If you do do this you might need to change the following line:

If self.tongue_dist == 0

To:

If self.tongue_dist < 0

If might never equal zero. If it starts at 200 and reduces by 30 in each loop (as it would if self.tongue_extend equalled -3) it will jump right over zero.

Another reason to create a new fly

At the moment the flies are created here:

```
if (fly == None or time.time() > fly.spawn_time + 4.4):
    fly = Fly()
```

We described this line on page 216. It basically says the a new fly will be created if fly is equal to None, as is the case for the first fly created, or if the current fly has existed for more than 4.4 seconds. When a new fly is created the old fly is automatically destroyed. We don't have to program that.

But now the game has changed. We only want the fly to respawn after 4.4 seconds if it hasn't stuck to the tongue. So let's add that condition to the respawn line:

```
if fly == None or (time.time() > fly.spawn_time + 4.4 and not fly.stuck):
    fly = Fly()
```

Now we're going to write a second if statement for when the fly is stuck to the tongue. Place it directly after the statement above.

```
if fly.stuck and frog.tongue_dist == 0:
    fly = Fly()
```

If the fly has stuck to the tongue we want it to respawn after it's been eaten by the frog. We could say it has been eaten by the frog once the tongue has completely withdrawn. That's when the frog's **tongue_dist** is equal to 0.

We could write the two statements above as one if statement. We could bracket up the conditions in the first if statement, then place an **or**, then bracket the conditions in the second if statement and place them after the **or**. But we're not going to do this because we're going to deal with the frog's energy levels in the second statement (see page 234).

So now we're creating a new fly at the beginning of the game, or after 4.4 seconds has lapsed, or if the fly has been swallowed.

JUST BECAUSE YOU CAN DO SOMETHING DOESN'T MEAN YOU SHOULD.

Chapter twenty

In game statistics...

An energy bar

We're going to place a bar on to the top left of the screen to show the frog's energy level. This bar will go down as time goes on, until eventually the frog dies from starvation and the game is over. But every time the frog catches a fly it gains energy and the bar goes up.

```
pygame.draw.rect(screen,(200,50,0),(10,10,20,100))
```

This will place the bar at coordinates (10,10). It will be 20 pixels wide and a 100 pixels high. It's color will be (200,50,0) in rgb.

Place this line right after the fly.draw() function call in the game loop.

We want the height to change as energy levels change so instead of making the rectangle 100 pixels high, let's make a variable called **energy** and make **energy** equal a 100. Add the following line to the frog's __init__() function:

```
self.energy = 100
```

Now replace the **100** in the pygame.draw.rect() function above to **frog.energy**.

Then in the game loop we can reduce energy with each loop of the program. The following line can go anywhere in the **menu = "game"** section but think about what's neatest. We placed ours on the first line after **if menu = "game"**.

```
frog.energy -= 0.1
```

Now when you run the program and you'll see a bar that shrinks with time. Unfortunately it's upside down because y goes positive as it goes down the screen.

The best way to fix this is to change the **pygame.draw.rect()** function as follows:

```
pygame.draw.rect(screen,(200,50,0),(10,110,20,-frog.energy))
```

Pygame allows you to draw shapes with negative sizes. In reality this just means extend in the opposite direction from the coordinates. So here we've created a rectangle at (10,110) that extends upwards. Its height is -100 pixels. As **energy** decreases the height will come down.

Note: the value of energy is a float because we're reducing it by 0.1 each game loop but, unlike the **draw.circle()** function, the **draw.rect()** function can cope with this. If this is causing a problem replace **-frog.energy** with **-int(frog.energy)**.

When energy goes below zero the rectangle starts growing again in the opposite direction. We'll fix this by placing the draw.rect() function in an if statement:

```
if frog.energy >= 0:
    pygame.draw.rect(screen,(200,50,0),(10,110,20,-frog.energy))
```

Now if energy drops to zero or below the rectangle won't be drawn at all.

IF MY ENERGY GOES TO ZERO I WON'T BE DRAWN AT ALL?

When the frog swallows a fly we need to give it an energy boost. We want to see the energy bar go up. We have a place in the game loop where the fly is swallowed so we just need to add a line to boost the energy:

```
if fly.stuck and frog.tongue_dist == 0:
    frog.energy = min(100, frog.energy+50)
    fly = Fly()
```

The min() function returns the lowest value in the brackets. So energy will either be made equal to 100 or have 50 added to its current value, whichever is lower. In this way the energy level can never go over a 100.

Survival time.

Let's add a clock to the screen to show how long we've stayed alive. We already have the time module loaded so we don't have to worry about that. Let's create a variable called **game_start**. This sets the time when the game starts so it needs to go where the game is triggered by a mouse click on the start button.

```
if pygame.mouse.get_pressed()[0] and buttonrect.collidepoint(pygame.mouse.get_pos()):
    menu = "game"
    game_start = time.time()
```

We'll need to add a font into the set up with which to write the clock:

```
font2 = pygame.font.SysFont("couriernew",15)
```

Then add the following lines into the game loop, maybe after the code the creates the energy bar.

```
txt = font2.render("Time:"+str(int((time.time()-game_start)*10)/10.),True,(0,0,0))
screen.blit(txt,(10,120))
```

time.time() - game_start gives us the current game time. We multiply it by ten, turn it into an integer and then divide by 10.0 to make it a float to 1 decimal place. We showed you this trick on page 115. There is a function in Python that rounds numbers to a particular decimal place but this method is easier and cooler. We've blitted the txt underneath the energy bar though you might want to place it elsewhere on the screen.

It is possible the fly could land under the energy bar. To prevent this we could move the calling of the fly's draw() function to after the drawing of the bar and the blitting of the clock. Then the fly will be blitted on top of the energy bar should the random coordinates place it on that area of the screen. Or we could change the where the fly is allowed to land by changing the coordinates selected in the fly's __init__() function:

```
self.x = random.randint(50,screen.get_width()-fly_image.get_width())
```

Now the fly isn't allowed to land in the left hand 50 pixels of the screen.

Another way to die

We thought we'd make the frog shrink to nothing when the game is over. The condition for game over is that the frog has to have no energy left. When the game is over two things are going to happen. First the frog is going to shrink to nothing. Let's make that happen over two seconds. Then we're going to put up a game over screen with a score of some kind.

So first we need to mark the time when the frog runs out of energy. We'll create a variable called **death_time**. We've placed this variable in the set up but it could go in the class just as we did with energy. The choice is yours. Neither variable is used in the class but if there were two or more frogs they would need to go in the class because they'd need to be associated with a specific frog.

```
death_time = False
```

We'll talk about why we've made **death_time** equal to False on page 237

Then we need to mark when the frog runs out of energy.

```
if frog.energy <= 0:
    death_time = time.time()
```

These lines can go right after the other if statement dealing with energy in the game loop.

There's a major problem here. Energy is going to be less than or equal to zero on the next loop and every loop after that, which means **death_time** will keep resetting to time.time(). We only want this to happen once, when energy first goes to zero or below. So we need to write:

```
if frog.energy <= 0 and not death_time:
    death_time = time.time()
```

AHH!

I'M DOOMED

In the statement on the previous page we've added in the condition that **death_time** is not True. This might seem strange given that most of the time **death_time** is going to be a very large number (time.time()). We've said before that 0 is False and 1 is True. Well, this isn't quite the whole truth. 0 will always be considered False, but any other number, not just 1, will return a True. This is even the case with things like lists. An empty list is False, a list with things in it is True.

If **death_time** returns a True then **not death_time** will return a False and the second condition in the if statement won't be met. So if **death_time** is set to **time.time()** then this if statement won't trigger again.

This all means that **death_time** has to be False before this if statement gets used for the first time. This is why, when we created **death_time** in the set up, we made it equal to False. We could have made it equal to 0, this would work just the same, but but it seems sensible to call it False in this case.

WHAT'S WRONG?

AREN'T YOU GOING TO KILL ME?
ISN'T THIS DEATH TIME?

We said we were going to make the frog shrink to nothing when it starves. This is going to be done in the draw() function. In pseudo code the draw() function will look like this:

IF DEATH_TIME RETURNS A TRUE

    SHRINK THE FROG

ELSE

    DO THE NORMAL STUFF WITH THE ROTATION AND THE TONGUE.

Here's the actual code:

```
def draw(self):
    if death_time:
        rotated = pygame.transform.rotozoom(frog_image,self.dir,1-((time.time()-death_time)/2))
        screen.blit(rotated,(screen.get_width()/2-rotated.get_width()/2,
            screen.get_height()/2-rotated.get_height()/2))
    else:
        tpos = self.get_tongue_pos()
        pygame.draw.circle(screen,(255,50,50),tpos,10)
        pygame.draw.line(screen,(255,50,50),(screen.get_width()/2,
            screen.get_height()/2),tpos,10)
        rotated = pygame.transform.rotate(frog_image,self.dir)
        screen.blit(rotated,(screen.get_width()/2-rotated.get_width()/2,
            screen.get_height()/2-rotated.get_height()/2))
```

DO YOU WANT
TO KILL ME?

WELL, KIND OF.

To shrink the frog we're going to use Pygame's **rotozoom()** function. Like **rotate()**, **rotozoom()** is in the transform module. It both rotates and zooms in or out of an image. It takes three arguments: an image; the rotation in degrees; and a scaler which multiples the dimensions of the image. Let's look at that third argument.

```
1-((time.time()-death_time)/2)
```

When **death_time** first returns a true and this argument is first used **death_time** will be equal to **time.time()**. So **time.time() - death_time** will be zero. A half of zero is still zero. So this line will will give us 1-0, which is 1. So the the dimensions of the image will be multiplied by 1. It will say the same size.

A half second later **time.time() - death_time** will give us 0.5. 0.5/2 gives us 0.25. 1-0.25 gives us 0.75. So the the dimensions of the image will be multiplied by 0.75.

A full second later **time.time() - death_time** will give us 1. 1/2 gives us 0.5. 1-0.5 gives us 0.5. So the the dimensions of the image will be multiplied by 0.5.

Two seconds later **time.time() - death_time** will give us 2. 2/2 gives us 1. 1-1 gives us 0. So the the dimensions of the image will be multiplied by 0. The image will disappear.

You can see that the divisor in the argument above, the 2, will be the number of seconds it takes for the image to shrink to nothing. You could replace it with a different value if you want the frog to shrink slower or quicker.

We've called the new image created by rotozoom(): **rotated**. This transformed image is then blitted to the centre of the screen in the next line. We've seen this before.

OH. WELL, IN THAT CASE...

NO. NO. I ONLY WANT TO KILL YOU TO STOP YOU FROM KILLING ME.

There is something a little strange that can happen. If the frog dies when its tongue is out the frog shrinks but the tongue simply disappears because the part of the draw() function dealing with the tongue is no longer being run. To fix this we're simply going to delay the frog shrinking until after the tongue has withdrawn. This time lag won't be noticed in the game. We can do this by adding the condition that the tongue is withdrawn into the if statement triggering the change in death_time.

```
if energy <= 0 and not death_time and frog.tongue_dist == 0:
    death_time = time.time()
```

YOU KNOW, YOU GUYS
ARE WEIRD. COME
ON, KITTY. LET'S GO.

Finally we want a game over screen. In the space invader and pong games we created the game over screen in a while loop inside the game loop. Here we're going to use the Menu variable. Either way is fine; it's up you you to pick the methods you want to use.

So in pseudo code we're going to add a section like this:

IF MENU = "DEAD"

    BLIT THE GAME OVER SCREEN

    BLIT THE SCORE AND ANY STATS

    CREATE A RESTART BUTTON

    IF RESTART BUTTON CLICKED

        RESET THE GAME VARIABLES

        MENU = "GAME"

Before we do this we need to have a place where menu gets set to "dead". This will happen when the frog has shrunk to nothing, which will be 2 seconds after the frog starved. When the frog starved we set **death_time** to **time.time()** (page 236) so we can write this line:

```
if time.time() > death_time + 2:
    menu = "dead"
```

This line can be the last line before the display update.

There is a major problem with this line. It looks like it should work but if we use it like this menu will be set to "dead" the moment we start the game. We'll never get a chance to play. If you look at where the **death_time** variable was created in the set up part of the program you might see the problem. **death_time = False**. Well, False is the same as Zero and time.time() is always going to be greater than 0+2.

To fix this we can take advantage of the fact that when death_time is set to time.time() it not only gets that value, it also goes from being False to being True. If **death_time** is False we don't want the if statement above to trigger. Put another way if **death_time** is True then allow the if statement to trigger. Like so:

```
if death_time and time.time() > death_time + 2:
    menu = "dead"
```

Now **death_time** has to be True; that is, it has to have a value other than zero or False, for menu to be set to "dead".

Now we can look at what happens when menu is equal to "dead". First we need to load our game over screen in the set up part of the program. We've used an image the same size as the screen called **flycatcher_game_over**. Downloadable from the website as always. So we need to add the following line into the set up:

```
gameover_image = pygame.image.load("images/flycatcher_game_over.png").convert_alpha()
```

The game over screen appears as below. The fly is in the game over image but the button and the survival time are added in the code.

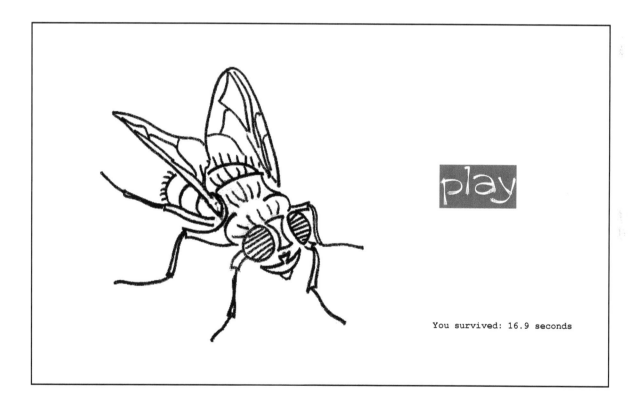

```
if menu == "dead":
    screen.blit(gameover_image,(0,0))
    txt = font2.render(
↵       "You survived: "+str(int((death_time - game_start)*10)/10.)+"seconds",True,(0,0,0))
    screen.blit(txt,(705,500))
    txt = font.render("Play",True,(255,255,255))
    txt_x = 705
    txt_y = 235
    buttonrect = pygame.Rect((txt_x,txt_y),txt.get_size())
    pygame.draw.rect(screen,(200,50,0),buttonrect)
    screen.blit(txt, (txt_x, txt_y))

    if pygame.mouse.get_pressed()[0] and buttonrect.collidepoint(pygame.mouse.get_pos()):
        menu = "game"
        game_start = time.time()
        energy = 100
        death_time = False
        fly = None
        frog = Frog()
```

Now we can look at what happens when the menu gets set to "dead". Make sure you get the indent correct. The "if menu" lines up under the other "if menu"s. They have the same indent as the display update. This section can go last thing before the display update.

First of all the game_over image gets blitted to the screen. We blit the time the player survived over the top of the image. The time a player survived is going to be **death_time - game_start**.

We also blit a restart button in exactly the same way we blitted the start button on page 211. It's in a slightly different position but is otherwise identical. When the button is clicked, menu is reset to "game" and all the conditions of the game are reset to their starting values.

We still have a minor problem here. The clock keeps on running after the frog has starved. It would be nice if it stopped as soon as energy went to zero. At the moment the lines dealing with the on screen clock (page 235) look like this:

```
txt = font.render("Time:"+str(int((time.time()-game_start)*10)/10.),True,(0,0,0))
screen.blit(txt,(10,120))
```

We want the time, given by **time.time()-game_start**, to freeze once the frog's energy has gone to zero. So let's change the two lines above to the following:

```
if death_time:
    txt = font.render("Time:"+str(int((death_time - game_start)*10)/10.),True,(0,0,0))
else:
    txt = font.render("Time:"+str(int((time.time() - game_start)*10)/10.),True,(0,0,0))
screen.blit(txt,(10,120))
```

When the game begins death_time returns a False so the **else:** part of the statement above will be returned. That's exactly what we had before. The time will be blitted onto the screen at the coordinate (10,120). But if **death_time** returns a True, as when the frog's energy goes to zero, then the top lines kicks in. **txt** will be set to the final time, that is **death_time - game_start**, in the same font and to the same position as the game clock. When this version of **txt** is blitted it will look as if the clock has simply stopped.

And that's the fly catcher game done. Eating flies has been fun but now we're going to get into a real battle.

The classic programming joke

WHY DOESN'T IT WORK?

PING!

WHY DOES IT WORK?

Chapter twenty-one

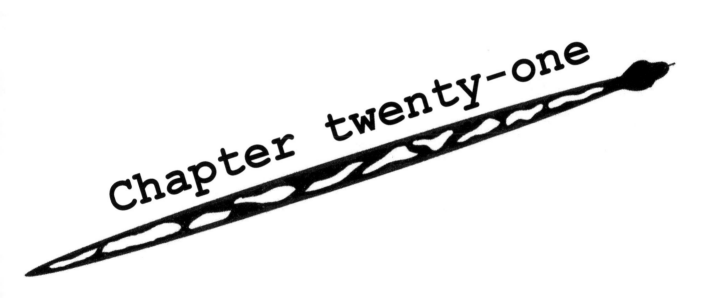

Having a blast...

Now we're going to build a new game. This will bring together the knowledge we've already gained, though we will introduce a few new things along the way just to keep it interesting. The game is a 2D tank battle for two players.

There are six images we're going to use:

> A start menu image. (Totally over the top. Drawn in paint.net with additional non copyrighted images found using Google. 1000 x 600 pixels)
> A wall. (Actually a tiny section from photo of some rooftops. 200 x 15 pixels)
> A second wall image. (This is just the wall above rotated. 15 x 200 pixels)
> 2 tanks. (Drawn in paint.net. 62 x 81 pixels)
> A landscape. (A small section of a desert landscape. 1000 x 600 pixels)

So let's get a basic program going with these images. We'll also set a caption, set the clock tick and program a start and game menu. You should be able to understand most of this just by reading through it but we are going to use a slightly different technique to create and deal with the start button. The images are available for download from the website or you can create your own. You should create your own. It's your game you're building and you want to give it your own look.

```
import pygame, sys
from pygame.locals import *
pygame.init()
pygame.display.set_caption("Tank Battle")
clock = pygame.time.Clock()
screen = pygame.display.set_mode((1000,600))
homescreen_image = pygame.image.load("images/TBhomescreen.jpg").convert()
landscape_image = pygame.image.load("images/landscape.jpg").convert()
wall_image = pygame.image.load("images/wall.png").convert()
vert_wall_image = pygame.transform.rotate(wall_image,90)
tankG_image = pygame.image.load("images/tankG.png").convert_alpha()
tankB_image = pygame.image.load("images/tankB.png").convert_alpha()
menu = "home"

while 1:
    clock.tick(60)

    for event in pygame.event.get():
        if event.type == QUIT:
            sys.exit()

    if menu == "home":
        screen.blit(homescreen_image,(0,0))
        buttonrect = pygame.Rect(409,440,147,147)
        if pygame.mouse.get_pressed()[0] and
                    buttonrect.collidepoint(pygame.mouse.get_pos()):
            menu = "game"

    if menu == "game":
        screen.blit(landscape_image,(0,0))

    pygame.display.update()
```

When the start button is pressed all that will happen is the landscape image will load.

Our home_screen image already has a start button drawn onto it. In the Fly Catcher game we created a button using a colored rectangle with some text blitted over it. Here we've simply drawn the button onto the home screen image.

We need to know the coordinates and the size of the play button so we can detect if that area of the screen has been clicked on. To find the coordinates of the play button we can open the image in paint.net. In the toolbar at the bottom of the page paint.net gives you the coordinates of the mouse so it's easy to find the coordinates at a particular point on an image. (You might have to select the pixel option.)

Our start button is a circle but we can only use rectangles for the actual area of the screen we're going to click on -there's no circle equivalent of pygame.Rect(). So the clickable area will actually be the white box in the image below.

The top left of our play button is at (409,440). It's 147 pixels wide and 147 pixels high. We use these values to create an invisible rectangle using pygame.Rect(). Then collidepoint() checks to see if the mouse arrow is overlapping this rectangle.

Of course, the left mouse button has to be clicked as well for the menu to be set to "game".

This method of button creation is more straight forward than the one we used for Fly Catcher but it's useful to know both techniques.

A moving wall class

Now we'll create a wall class. The __init__ () function takes arguments for the position of each wall created and it's orientation. That's **x**, **y** and **vert** (short for vertical). This goes in the usual place for classes, after the set up.

```
class Wall:
    def __init__(self,x,y,vert):
        self.x = x
        self.y = y
        self.vert = vert

    def draw(self):
        if self.vert:
            screen.blit(vert_wall_image,(self.x,self.y))
        else:
            screen.blit(wall_image,(self.x,self.y))
```

vert will either be True or False. (You can see this from the lines below.) If **vert** returns a True then the vertical wall image will be blitted. Or else we get a False and the indented lines in the "else" section are followed.

We also need to create a list of walls. (Actually we're creating a tuple, hence the curved brackets.) And, as we did with the bats in Pong, we're going to create the wall instances here as well.

```
walls = (Wall(496,200,True),Wall(50,150,False),Wall(600,150,False),
        Wall(50,435,False),Wall(600,435,False))
```

And finally we have to call the draw() function.

```
for wall in walls:
    wall.draw()
```

We have several walls so we need a for loop. (No need for a while loop because we won't be deleting walls.) This line can go in the menu == "game" section of the game loop, after the landscape has been blitted. Remember, the for loop is indented inside the if menu == "game": statement.

There are some items in this picture we haven't got onto yet. And it's much better looking in color.

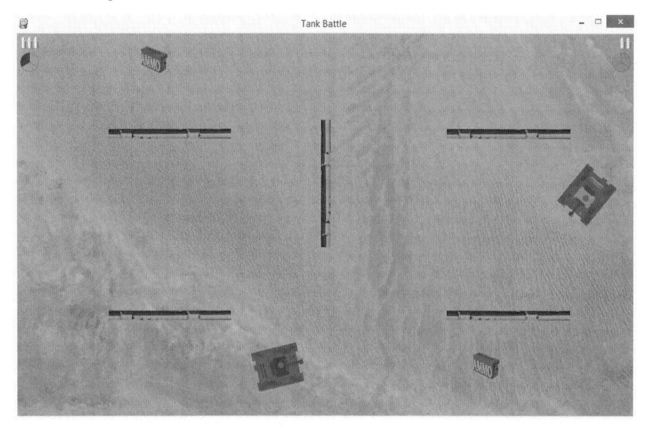

The horizontal walls use the same image. As you can see from the code, the vertical wall is a copy of the horizontal wall rotated. It would be possible to use only the horizontal wall image and to rotate it every time the vertical wall was needed. This would cut down on the number of images needed, generally a good thing, but asking Pygame to rotate the horizontal wall image every time the vertical wall was needed would be wasteful of processing power. It's best to have the two images.

Now we're going to persuade those walls to move.

The vertical wall is going to go up and down. This is very easy. We'll start it moving down and when it gets to a certain point we'll bounce it. The same if it goes too high. We would usually control vertical movement with a dy variable, but here we can use the same variable for the sideways movement of the horizontal walls so we'll just call the variable self.speed.

For the four horizontal walls we're going to divide the screen into no go zones.

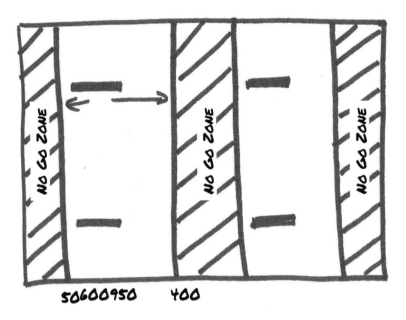

50600950   400

The walls bounce back and forth between the no go zones.

If a wall goes below x=50 or above x=950 then we'll bounce it. Or if it goes into that middle section where x is greater than 400 but less than 600, then we'll also bounce it. Remember the walls' coordinates are top left and the walls are 200 pixels wide so the actual numbers we use will take that into account.

Here's our psuedo code:

IF THE WALL IS VERTICAL

    MOVE THE WALL VERTICALLY BY SPEED.

IF THE WALL IS HORIZONTAL

    MOVE THE WALL HORIZONTALLY BY SPEED.

IF THE WALL IS EITHER(VERTICAL AND TOUCHING THE BOTTOM OR TOP NO GO ZONE) OR (HOZIZONTAL AND TOUCHING THE SIDE NO GO ZONES OR THE MIDDLE NO GO ZONE)

    REVERSE ITS DIRECTION

And here's the actual function:

```
def move(self):
    if self.vert:
        self.y+=self.speed
    else:
        self.x+=self.speed

    if (self.vert and (self.y < 50 or self.y > 350 )) or (not self.vert and
            ((self.x < 50 or self.x > 750) or (self.x > 200 and self.x <600 ))):
        self.speed*=-1
```

We've used the new variable **self.speed** so we need to add this variable into the Wall class's **__init__**() function.

```
def __init__(self,x,y,vert):
    self.x = x
    self.y = y
    self.vert = vert
    self.speed = 1
```

Of course, if you want the walls to move slower or faster you can change this value.

In the first section of the move() function we can see that if **self.vert** is True for a particular instance then we change **self.y** by **self.speed**. Or else (that is, if **self.vert** returns a False) we change **self.x** by **self.speed**. It is the horizontal walls that will return a False.

If you're struggling to see what's going on in the second section just keep comparing it to the pseudo code and it will become clear. There's a lot of boolean algebra but if you just work through it and look carefully at how the brackets open and close, it all makes sense.

The last thing is to call the move() function from the game loop:

```
for wall in walls:
    wall.move()
    wall.draw()
```

This line goes into the for loop controlling the walls, with the wall.draw() function. And now we have moving walls.

ISN'T A MOVING WALL A DOOR?

YOU CAN CALL THEM DOORS IF YOU LIKE. AND THE SHELLS THE TANKS ARE GOING TO FIRE ARE JUST ATOM REORGANISATION MODULES.

STUPID COMPUTER.

STUPID HUMAN.

Chapter twenty-two

War pigs...

A tank class

We have two tanks with two different images but we only need to build one class. So far all the images of a particular class have been identical but here we want to be able to tell each tank apart because they're going to be able to move all over the screen.

Let's start with the __init__() function. The tanks are going to take quite a few arguments. We need to set start coordinates, direction, controls and image.

```
class Tank:
    def __init__(self,x,y,dir,ctrls,img):
        self.x = x
        self.y = y
        self.ctrls = ctrls
        self.dir = dir
        self.img = img
```

We've seen most of these arguments before, but img is new. This is here because, as with the other arguments, each tank will have its own image.

The tanks are created in the usual place after the classes:

```
tankG = Tank(740,20,180,(K_UP,K_DOWN,K_LEFT,K_RIGHT),tankG_image)
tankB = Tank(200,500,0,(K_w,K_s,K_a,K_d),tankB_image)
```

We've done something silently different here. We've created each instance separately. This means we can give each tank a name, rather that have it identified by it's position in the list like we did with the walls and the pong bats (page 126 and 250). Either way is perfectly valid. We've done it this way to show you that it can be done like this, but also because this ways makes things clearer later on.

tankG is the green tank, tankB is the blue.

You can see we have x, y and direction, followed by the controls, followed by the image.

Now, the draw() function:

```
def draw(self):
    rotated = pygame.transform.rotate(self.img,self.dir)
    screen.blit(rotated,(self.x+self.img.get_width()/2-rotated.get_width()/2,
        self.y+self.img.get_height()/2-rotated.get_height()/2))
```

This is almost identical to the draw() function we used for the rotating fighter in space invaders. Here we've had to grab the image from self.image because each tank is given its own image when it's created. It means we get objects with names like self.img.get_width() which seem to have a dot too many. But this is just fine.

We also need to call the draw() function from the game loop. Usually we've used a for loop that has gone through a list of instances. We did this for walls. This is a reason we usually use lists -it makes calling functions easier. But for the tanks we gave each a different name so we'll have to call the draw() function separately for each tank. We only have two tanks so it's not too much work. These lines can go right before the for loop that controls the walls.

```
tankG.draw()
tankB.draw()
```

Now we should have our two tanks sitting in their start positions. Next we need them to move around.

IT'S THE ONLY WAY I CAN GET THE
TANKS TO MOVE.

Rolling thunder

To move the tanks, first of all we need to detect key presses. We need to create our **pressed_keys** list in the usual place right after the quit section in the game loop.

```
pressed_keys = pygame.key.get_pressed()
```

We're using the math module so we have to import **math** on line 1. We'll also need **random**, and while we're at it we may as well add **time**, which we'll use later.

```
import pygame, sys, time, random, math
```

Then we can add the move() function to the Tank class:

```
def move(self):
    dx = math.sin(math.radians(self.dir))
    dy = math.cos(math.radians(self.dir))
    if pressed_keys[self.ctrls[0]]:
        self.x-=dx
        self.y-=dy
    if pressed_keys[self.ctrls[1]]:
        self.x+=0.5*dx
        self.y+=0.5*dy
    if pressed_keys[self.ctrls[2]]:
        self.dir+=1
    if pressed_keys[self.ctrls[3]]:
        self.dir-=1
```

We're going to be moving at angles so we're going to have to use **sohcohtoa** (page 140) to work out **dx** and **dy**. **self.dir** is in degrees because we were using it to rotate an image, so we have to convert it to radians. We're going to move the tank one pixel with every game loop so the "h" in our **sohcohtoa** equations is going to be 1. There's no need to type in "*1" in an equation because multiplying by 1 doesn't do anything.

dx and **dy** get created at the beginning of the function because they are used further down. They need creating before they are used. They're only used inside this function so they don't need a **self**.

We then have an if statement for each of the controls given to a tank when it was created. Here the first if statement is going move the tank by 1 pixel in the direction self.dir with each game loop. Of course there will be some rounding because dx and dy will usually be floats rather than integers but the coordinates you place an object at have to be in integers. The blit() function can cope with floats. It rounds them automatically.

In the second if statement, which is moving the tank backward, we've multiplied by 0.5. This means the tanks will move backward at half the speed they move forward. You can set your own speeds, of course.

You'll note that we're adding dx and dy to self.x and self.y to move backward and subtracting to move forward. Unlike the situation on page 194, we haven't placed a minus sign on the front of the math.sin() and math.cos() functions. But the situation is the same so we have to minus dy and dx when intuition says we should add, and vice versa. Either way is fine.

Then we have the third and fourth controls in the list of controls given when we created the tanks change self.dir and therefore the direction the tanks move in.

Now we need to call the move() function for each of the tanks:

```
tankG.move()
tankB.move()
```

These line go in the game loop inside the menu == "game" section. They could go right before the landscape is blitted. It's up to you.

Now we have some tanks that drive around the screen.

SO WHEN IT WASN'T
WORKING IT WAS ALL
MY FAULT.

SUDDENLY IT RUNS
LIKE A DREAM AND
SHE'S THE GENIUS.

Shells

Now we have a basic tank let's give it some weapons. After that we can refine the game with collision detection, lives and the like.

When we create a Shell class the shells will need to be given arguments for position and direction.

```
class Shell:
    def __init__(self,x,y,dir):
        self.dx = -math.sin(math.radians(dir))*5
        self.dy = -math.cos(math.radians(dir))*5
        self.x = x + self.dx * 8
        self.y = y + self.dy * 8

    def move(self):
        self.x += self.dx
        self.y += self.dy

    def draw(self):
        pygame.draw.circle(screen, (100,50,50), (int(self.x), int(self.y)), 3)
```

We'll be feeding the __init__() function x, y and dir. x and y will be the centre of the tank (see the shell constructor on page 263) and dir will be the direction of the tank.

Unlike the tank, we create the self.dx and self.dy variables in the __init__() function because they don't ever need recalculating. The same as for the dx and dy values for the missile and the badguy.

The shells are moving at 5 pixels per loop That's the *5. Deciding exactly what speed the shells should move at is really just trial and error. You might decide on a different speed.

As with the missiles on page 197, we've made it so the shells first appear just in front of the tank. That's the `self.dx*8` and the `self.dy*8`. **dx** and **dy** move the shell 5 pixels at the angle dir. For the initial self.x and self.y coordinates of the shell we're adding 8 times that to the **x** and **y** coordinates given by the tank's centre of rotation. So the shells will first appear 40 pixels from the centre of the tank. This will be well outside the area we're going to use for the collision detection between a shell and a tank.

Similarly to the fighter, this stops shells coming out skewed if we fire and rotate the tank at the same time, but there's a more important reason. Here if we get hit by a shell we lose a life. If we launch a shell from inside the tank the shell will be hitting the tank. This would be bad.

The **move()** function is nothing we haven't seen before.

In the **draw()** function we're just going to draw a circle using Pygame's circle drawing module. We covered this back on page 14. You could load an image but you're limited to something about 6 x 8 pixels so you can't draw much detail. The image will then get rotated, so much of what detail you do have will be lost.

Once we have the basic class done we need to create a list:

```
shells = []
```

For the walls and the two tanks we've created tuples because nothing inside the tuple changes during the game. For shells we need a list because we're going to be adding and deleting instances as we play. This can go in the same place we created the tanks and walls.

We need a loop in the game loop to call the shells. We're going to need to delete shells so it has to be a while loop. We first saw this with the raindrops on page 48.

```
i = 0
while i < len(shells):
    shells[i].move()
    shells[i].draw()
    i+=1
```

We'll add in shell deletion later because it's a little more complicated than we've seen before. These lines could go after the for loop controlling the walls.

We then need to create the shells using the shell constructor. This goes in a **fire()** function in the Tank class. (We're not at the point where we can create an instance of a class from inside that class yet.) So place the following lines in the Tank class.

```
    def fire(self):
        shells.append(Shell(self.x+self.img.get_width()/2,
                    self.y+self.img.get_height()/2,self.dir))
```

You can see from the shell's __init__() function that a shell takes the arguments, x, y and dir. These will be the tank's x-position minus half the width of the tank image, and the tank's y position minus half the height of the tank image (the two giving us the tank's centre of rotation), and the direction the tank is pointing in, that being self.dir.

The **fire()** function creates the shells but we have to call the function from somewhere. As with the missiles in space invaders we're going to place the key detection for the fire buttons in the quit section.

```
    for event in pygame.event.get():
        if event.type == QUIT:
            sys.exit()
        if event.type == KEYDOWN and event.key == K_RSHIFT and menu == "game":
            tankG.fire()
        if event.type == KEYDOWN and event.key == K_q and menu == "game":
            tankB.fire()
```

The shells should fire now.

You can see we've used the Right Shift key and the Q key as our fire buttons. Of course, you can choose different keys if you like. We have also made sure the shells can only fire if we're in the "game" menu. If we don't do this then shells can be created when we're in the start menu. They won't be drawn or move because these functions are only called when we're in "game" menu. But because they've been created then as soon as we switch to "game" menu they will fly across the screen. Delete the 'and menu == "game" from the lines above, press the fire buttons while in "start", switch to "game", and see what happens.

Let's do something slightly different with the shells. We're going to have them bounce off the walls and edges much like we had the pong ball bounce off the bats and top and bottom. We won't give any random bounce to the shells but we will give them a a maximum number of bounces, after which they disappear. So we're going to count the bounces. First we'll create a **bounce()** variable:

```
self.bounces = 0
```

This line goes into the shell's **__init__()** function.

Then create a **bounce()** function in the shell class. We're going to give you the whole lot at once but we think you'll be able to cope:

```
def bounce(self):
    for wall in walls:
        if wall.vert and pygame.Rect((wall.x,wall.y),
                vert_wall_image.get_size()).collidepoint(self.x,self.y):
            self.dx*=-1
            self.bounces += 1

        if not wall.vert and pygame.Rect((wall.x,wall.y),
                wall_image.get_size()).collidepoint(self.x,self.y):
            self.dy*=-1
            self.bounces += 1

    if self.x < 0 or self.x > 1000:
        self.dx*=-1
        self.bounces += 1

    if self.y < 0 or self.y > 600:
        self.dy*=-1
        self.bounces += 1
```

The **bounce()** function is in the Shell class so **self** refers to a particular shell. In pseudo code it looks like this:

FOR ANY WALL
   IF THE WALL IS VERTICAL AND COLLIDING WITH THE SHELL
      REVERSE THE SHELL'S DX AND ADD 1 TO THE NUMBER OF BOUNCES
   IF THE WALL IS HORIZONTAL AND COLLIDING WITH THE SHELL
      REVERSE THE SHELL'S DY AND ADD 1 TO THE NUMBER OF BOUNCES
IF THE SHELL HITS THE SIDES OF THE SCREEN
   REVERSE THE SHELL'S DX AND ADD 1 TO THE NUMBER OF BOUNCES
IF THE SHELL HITS THE TOP OR BOTTOM OF THE SCREEN
   REVERSE THE SHELL'S DY AND ADD 1 TO THE NUMBER OF BOUNCES

Remember, `wall.vert` returns either a True or False depending of the argument a particular wall was given. If `wall.vert` is False then the statement `not wall.vert` will return a True. (**not** simply reverses a True or False.)

That first if statement is saying that if the wall is vertical and a Rect placed at the same position as the wall and with the same dimensions as the wall is colliding with the shell (given by the coordinates of the shell) then reverse dx and add one to **self.bounces**.

The next if statement does the same for horizontal walls (that is: not vertical). It reverses dy and adds 1 to **self.bounces**.

These two if statements are in a for loop that goes through each wall in turn.

The third if statement asks if the shell is hitting either side of the screen. That is, where self.x is less than 0 or greater than 1000. If so dx is reversed, causing the shell to reverse its direction horizontally. And 1 added to **self.bounces**.

And the final if statement does the same for the top and bottom of the screen.

Now we have to call the **bounce()** function. This goes into the while loop controlling

```
i = 0
while i < len(shells):
    shells[i].move()
    shells[i].bounce()
    shells[i].draw()
    i+=1
```

If we run the code now we can fire shells and they will bounce. There's nothing destroying them yet, and they don't destroy the tanks, so we can fill the screen with them. There might be a game where doing this is a good thing, but not here.

You might also notice the shells sometimes get caught in the moving walls, much like the balls getting caught in the bats (page 149). We don't need to sort this problem because we're going to delete the shells after four bounces anyway.

Order of operations

In high school you were probably taught or will be taught bidmas to help you remember the order of mathematical operators. Thats's Brackets, Indices, Division, Multiplication, Addition, Subtracton.

So 2+3x4 is 14 not 20. (2+3)x4 is 20.

Using bidmas it's easy to think that 5-4+8 equals -7, after all you're meant to do addition before subtraction. But if you open a command line, load Python and try 5-4+8 Python will return 9, which is the correct answer. This is because additions are not really done before subtractions. Additions and subtractions actually done in order from left to right. It's true that all multiplications and divisions are done before all additions and subtractions, but once there are only additions and subtractions remaining they are done from left to right. This is also true of of divisions and multiplications. Divisions are not necessarily done before multiplications, they are worked through from left to right. To avoid this confusion programmers usually bracket things. This also makes it easier to read on the page.

Booleans also have an order of operations. For example:

　　　　not A or B.

Does this mean not(A or B) or does it mean (not A) or (B)?

The order of operations is <u>not</u> then <u>and</u> then <u>or</u>. So (not A) or (B) is correct.

We need to add in the code that deletes shells. We have several conditions where a shell should be deleted so we're going to use a **flag** (last seen on page 66). Basically we pin a flag to each shell and say that as long as the flag returns a False then the shell can keep on doing its thing. If the flag returns a True then the shell gets deleted.

Here we add the flag into the while loop that's controlling shells.

```
i = 0
while i < len(shells):
    shells[i].move()
    shells[i].bounce()
    shells[i].draw()

    flag = False

    if flag:
        del shells[i]
        i -= 1
    i += 1
```

Remember `if flag:` is asking if flag is True. Here, if flag is True we delete shell number **i** off the shell list.

HI MIKE. HAVEN'T SEEN YOU AROUND FOR A WHILE. I KIND OF MISSED YOU.

YOU MISSED ME? I THOUGHT YOU WERE MAD AT ME.

THE TWO AREN'T NECESSARILY MUTUALLY EXCLUSIVE.

Now we'll put in the conditions to make the flag true. They will be: if self.bounces reaches 5, if the shell hits tankG or if the shell hits tankB.

We're going to create a function in the tank class called **hit_shell()** to tell the tanks what to do when hit by a shell. We can use it in the while loop controlling the shells, as shown below. We'll build the **hit_shell()** function on the next page.

```
i = 0
while i < len(shells):
    shells[i].move()
    shells[i].bounce()
    shells[i].draw()

    flag = False

    if tankG.hit_shell(shells[i]):
        flag = True

    if tankB.hit_shell(shells[i]):
        flag = True

    if shells[i].bounces == 5:
        flag = True

    if flag:
        del shells[i]
        i -= 1
    i += 1
```

Here we can see that if the **hit_shell()** function returns a True then the shell's flag gets set to True. The same happens if **bounces** gets to 5. If we get a True then the shell gets deleted.

Here's the collision detection between a shell and a tank. This function goes in the tank class.

```
def hit_shell(self,shell):
    return pygame.Rect(self.x,self.y+10,60,60).collidepoint(shell.x,shell.y)
```

We've given the virtual rectangle that gets placed over the tank a y coordinate of self.y + 10. This is because the Rect stays still as the tank rotates and we want it to be inside the tank whatever the tank's rotation. We've created a square that will be inside the tank if it's pointing up or sideways and only a little out of the tank is pointing and an angle. We can't make the Rect rotate so it has to work for whatever direction the tank is pointing in. Making perfect collision detection is too complicated for this book but we can make something plenty good enough.

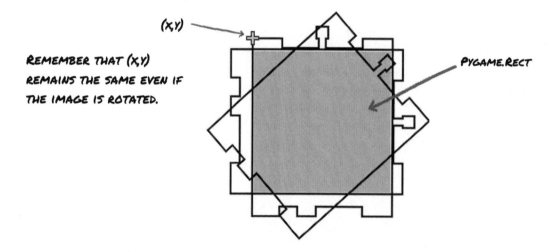

(x,y)

REMEMBER THAT (X,Y) REMAINS THE SAME EVEN IF THE IMAGE IS ROTATED.

PYGAME.RECT

You can always make the pygame.Rect smaller and shift it's coordinates to bring it completely inside the tank when the tank is at an angle. But then shells hitting the edges of the tanks won't count as a hit. As always, it's a compromise.

At the moment the shell will bounce 4 times but be deleted if it bounces again, and it will be deleted if it hits a tank. But the tanks aren't suffering.

Causing harm

Now let's build the **harm()** function. When a tank gets hit it's going to flash for a couple of seconds and lose a life. While it's flashing it's going to be immune to any further hits. We're going to use a **lives** variable as well as one called **flash_time_end** so we need to create these variables:

```
self.flash_time_end = 0
self.lives = 3
```

These lines go into the __init__() function of the Tank class.

Now the add the following function into the Tank class:

```
def harm(self):
    if time.time() > self.flash_time_end:
        self.flash_time_end = time.time() + 2
        self.lives -= 1
```

Make sure you've imported the **time** module in the first line of the program.

The function gets called when a shell collides with a tank, that is when **hit_shell()** returns a True. Let's look at what happens. If the current time is greater than **flash_time_end** then we get a True. That's going to happen for sure because **flash_time_end** is equal to zero. Then we make **flash_time_end** equal to **time.time()** plus 2. That means that if the **harm()** function gets called anytime in the next 2 seconds that first if statement won't be true; **time.time()** will be less than **self.flash_time_end**. So we won't reset **flash_time_end** and we won't lose another life. After two seconds though, we're back to losing a life because that if statemeant will return a True.

Finally we need to call the harm() function when a tank gets hit.

```
if tankG.hit_shell(shells[i]):
    tankG.harm()
    flag = True

if tankB.hit_shell(shells[i]):
    tankB.harm()
    flag = True
```

We're calling from inside the while loop that controls the shells. Now when a collision between and tank and shell is detected, not only does the shell have its flag changed, but the tank's **harm()** function gets called.

Flashing

We haven't actually made the tank flash yet. We'll do that in the tank's draw() function.

```
def draw(self):
    if time.time() > self.flash_time_end or time.time()%0.1 < 0.05:
        rotated = pygame.transform.rotate(self.img,self.dir)
        screen.blit(rotated, (self.x+self.img.get_width()/2-rotated.get_width()/2,
                self.y+self.img.get_height()/2-rotated.get_height()/2))
```

We've added in an if statement that's spilt into two conditions separated by an **or**. So only one condition has to be True for the screen blit to happen. Well, the first condition is going to give a True almost all of the time. The only time it isn't is for that two second period right after the **harm()** function is called. This means that apart from those two seconds the tank is definitely going to be drawn.

Let's look at: `time.time()%0.1 < 0.05:`

We used modulus before when we were dealing with angles. We described modulus there, but another way of thinking of modulus is as the remainder of a sum. 17÷3 is 5 remainder 2. So 17 mod 3 is 2. In Python we would write `17%3`to get that answer 2. The answer is always going to be between 0 and the number you're using to divide with (the divisor).

In the line above **time.time() % 0.1** is going to be between 0 and 0.1. For half of the time it will be less than 0.05. When this is the case we get a true and the tank gets blitted. Otherwise we get a false and the tank isn't blitted. This is a common way of making an image flash.

Mess around with getting things to flash in different ways. For example, in the first program we wrote back on page 1 if we place the line that draws the circle in an if statement like this:

```
if time.time() % 1 < 0.5:
    pygame.draw.circle(screen,(0,255,0),(100,150),20)
```

You will have to load the time module in the first line.

Try `if time.time() % 1 < 0.2:`

Or `if time.time() % 2 < 1.7:`

You could replace a number with a variable and make it change with each game loop. There's an example on the website.

More sound effects

It would be nice if we could hear those shells hitting the tank. And maybe also hear the sound of the shells being fired. Let's add two sound effects. You'll need to download the sounds from the website and place them in your sounds folder. Or create your own, of course. The sounds are called **shell.ogg** and **tank_hit.ogg**.

In the program we need to load the sounds in the setup, like so:

```
shell_sound = pygame.mixer.Sound("sounds/shell.ogg")
harm_sound = pygame.mixer.Sound("sounds/tank_hit.ogg")
```

harm_sound needs to be called when a shell hits a tank. That will be here:

```
    if tankG.hit_shell(shells[i]):
        tankG.harm()
        harm_sound.play()
        flag = True

    if tankB.hit_shell(shells[i]):
        tankB.harm()
        harm_sound.play()
        flag = True
```

shell_sound can to triggered when a shell is created in the shell's __init__() function:

```
    def __init__(self,x,y,dir):
        self.dx = -math.sin(math.radians(dir))*5
        self.dy = -math.cos(math.radians(dir))*5
        self.x = x + self.dx * 8
        self.y = y + self.dy * 8
        self.bounces = 0
        shell_sound.play()
```

However, when you play the game you'll notice the sound is delayed by a noticeable amount. The shells are fired then the sound comes a few hundred milliseconds late. This is because pygame loads sounds into a buffer before playing them. There are good reasons for this but here it's annoying. To solve this we shrink the buffer. Place the following line in the set up before the pygame.init() line. This is important.

```
pygame.mixer.init(buffer=512)
```

Now the sound won't lag.

Solid walls

At the moment our tanks can drive through the walls. We need to stop that happening. First some collision detection between the tanks and the walls. In pseudo code this is what we're going to do:

FIND IF THE FOLLOWING GIVES A TRUE OR FALSE

VERTICAL OVERLAPPING WITH THE TANK

OR

NOT VERTICAL OVERLAPPING WITH THE TANK

```
def hit_wall(self,wall):
    return wall.vert and
        pygame.Rect((wall.x,wall.y),vert_wall_image.get_size()).colliderect((self.x,self.y+10),(60,60))
        or (not wall.vert and
        pygame.Rect((wall.x,wall.y),wall_image.get_size()).colliderect(self.x,self.y+10,60,60))
```

The **hit_wall()** function is in the Tank class so the **self** refers to a tank. It's going to be called from the for loop controlling the walls so each wall is going to be fed to it in turn (page 274).

We're using **colliderect()** here so we're looking for collisions between two rectangles. **Rect()** and **colliderect()** are each taking two arguments, those being the coordinates and size of either the wall or the tank. The wall for **Rect()** and the tank for **colliderect()**.

All the conditions will return a True or a False. For example wall.vert will return a False if the wall is horizontal. In fact, we wrote in the True or False ourselves on page 250.

For the other three conditions in the **hit_wall()** function Python as to put in some effort and actually work something out. If either the first two **or** the second two are both True then the **hit_wall()** function will return a True. On page 270 you can see that if the **hit_shell()** function returns a True the **harm()** function will be called. On page 274 a True from the **hit_wall()** function also causes the **harm()** function to be called. Now either a shell hitting a tank or the tank hitting a wall will call the **harm()** function. The tank will lose a life and gain immunity from further loss for a couple of seconds.

This means that for those two seconds the tank will be able to drive though a wall or get hit again by a shell without suffering further loss of lives. We think this is okay and could be part of a battle strategy. Making the game so the tank can't drive through the wall but doesn't carry on losing lives is a little more complicated because both the tank and the wall are moving. It would be easy if the walls were still. We'll try and cover this kind of collision in the next book.

Now we need to call the **hit_wall()** function:

```
for wall in walls:
    wall.move()
    wall.draw()
    if tankG.hit_wall(wall):
        tankG.harm()

    if tankB.hit_wall(wall):
        tankB.harm()
```

We're in the for loop going through the list of walls. First we move and draw a wall then we check for collisions between tanks and the wall we're working on from the walls list. For tankG we see if **hit_wall()** returns a true. If it does we call the **harm()** function. We then do the same for tankB. And then onto the next wall in the walls list until they're all done.

YOUR LAPTOP'S ON FIRE AND THE FLAMES ARE SPREADING!

I KNOW. AS SOON AS I SAW THE SMOKE I BEGAN WRITING AN APP THAT DETECTS FIRE AND AUTOMATICALLY CALLS THE FIRE BRIGADE. I'M ALMOST FINISHED.

DAMMIT. COMPUTER JUST CRASHED.

There's nothing in a name

Note that the wall in brackets in the tankG.hit_wall(wall) is the wall from the for loop. Back on page 42 we said we could write a for loop like this:

```
for pepperoni in walls
    pepperoni.move()
    pepperoni.draw()
```

And follow it up with:

```
if tankG.hit_wall(pepperoni):
    tankG.harm()
if tankB.hit_wall(pepperoni):
    tankB.harm()
```

The hit_wall() function begins with the line:

```
def hit_wall(self,wall):
```

This would still work just fine because the word wall isn't related to the wall in the for loop. In fact the hit_wall() function could look like this:

```
def hit_wall(self,chicken):
    return (chicken.vert and ETC.
```

Python doesn't care about the names. All it wants in the information that gets carried along with the names. Anything in the list walls has three arguments -x,y and vert. These were given to the items in the list because everything in that list is of the Wall class and the Wall class has three arguments. These three arguments are handed to any pepperoni in the for loop. When the pepperoni gets passed to the hit_wall() function the hit_wall() function shrugs and says, I'm going to call you a chicken. All it really cares about is what's in the argument bag. It's hoping there's going to be an x, a y and a vert because that's what the function uses. If there isn't then Python will get upset and crash. It couldn't care less about the name of the thing carrying the arguments.

We hope this makes some sense. If it doesn't it really doesn't matter.

Lives

We have a **lives** variable but we haven't done anything with it. We could display **lives** in much the same way we displayed score in the pong game. We'd start with value, say 3, and then minus one off **lives** every time the tank got hit. We'd create a font, turn the value of the variable **lives** into a string, render it in the font and blit it to the screen. Instead we're going to represent **lives** as a graphic. We have a circle and we're going to remove a third every time a life is lost.

Like this:

This means a total of six images, three for each tank. We have a green set and a blue set. We're going to load the images in the usual place in the set up part of the program, but we're going to load them as two tuples:

```
G_lives=(
          pygame.image.load("images/lives_1G.png").convert_alpha(),
          pygame.image.load("images/lives_2G.png").convert_alpha(),
          pygame.image.load("images/lives_3G.png").convert_alpha()
        )
B_lives=(
          pygame.image.load("images/lives_1B.png").convert_alpha(),
          pygame.image.load("images/lives_2B.png").convert_alpha(),
          pygame.image.load("images/lives_3B.png").convert_alpha()
        )
```

We've written them like this in the code to keep everything neat on the screen but you'll note that Python is reading the above as just two lines. Tuples have to have parenthesis around them anyway. Python always reads anything in parenthesis as one line no matter how they're written on the screen.

Now place the following lines in the game loop. Where you place these lines depends on whether you want the tanks and shells to go over the score, or for the score to always be visible over the shells and tanks. We've put the score on top so these lines are going directly before the display update.

```
screen.blit(G_lives[tankG.lives-1],(965,30))
screen.blit(B_lives[tankB.lives-1],(5,30))
```

Here we're blitting items off the lives image lists we created on the previous page at a particular coordinate. The item number corresponds to the number of lives a tank has minus 1. That's because the image lists go from 0 to 2, and lives goes from 1 to 3.

Although the images are stored in a tuple we still use square brackets to fetch them. If we used parenthesis **G_lives** ands **B_lives** would look like functions.

WE'VE HAD A LOT OF ADVENTURES, HAVEN'T WE.

SURE HAVE. AND WE DON'T EVEN KNOW ABOUT SOME OF THEM.

HOW DO YOU MEAN?

ERM. WELL, WHEN I FIXING MY COMPUTER AFTER THE FIRE I FOUND SOME STRANGE CODE. IT LOOKS LIKE I MADE A RESET BUTTON. I THINK WE MIGHT HAVE HAD SOME OF OUR EXISTENCE WIPED OUT. BY THE WAY, DO YOU KNOW SOMEONE CALLED ANNA?

Game over

If you play the game just now you'll notice that when lives goes to zero, and Python should be fetching item -1 on the list, the 3 lives image gets blitted (that's item number 2). Python will allow this to happen until you reach minus the length of the list. Then it will complain that you're outside the list and crash.

We're never going to get that far. When a tank's lives drop to zero we're going to stop the game and declare a winner.

For this game we've decided to create two game over images, one for green winning, one for blue. They're the same size as the screen. You should, of course, create your own. But ours are available for download from the website.

First, load the game over images into the setup part of the program.

```
G_wins = pygame.image.load("images/greenwins.jpg").convert()
B_wins = pygame.image.load("images/bluewins.jpg").convert()
```

We need to place the following lines at the end of the game loop, directly before the display update:

```
if tankG.lives == 0:
    screen.blit(B_wins,(0,0))
    menu = "dead"

if tankB.lives == 0:
    screen.blit(G_wins,(0,0))
    menu = "dead"
```

If a player's lives go to zero the game over screen for the other player winning gets blitted and the menu gets set to "dead".

ANNA? NO. I DON'T KNOW ANYONE BY THAT NAME.

I JUST FOUND A FILE ON MY COMPUTER BUT IT'S BEEN CORRUPTED. THERE'S A NOTE THAT SAYS, "DEAR MIKE, ANNA IS SO CO..." THAT'S ALL.

Here's a black and white version of one of our game over screens.

The image is 1000 pixels by 600 pixels. As ever, top left is at 0,0. Top left of the play again button is at 555,444. It's 333 pixels wide and 88 pixels high. You can see these numbers in the code on the following page where we create the **Rect** that the mouse arrow has to overlap to restart the game.

MAYBE SHE'S SO COOL.

YEAH. MAYBE.

Here's the **menu == "dead"** if statement:

```
if menu == "dead":
    if pygame.mouse.get_pressed()[0] and
            pygame.Rect((555,444),(333,88)).collidepoint(pygame.mouse.get_pos()):
        shells = []
        tankG = Tank(740,20,180,(K_UP,K_DOWN,K_LEFT,K_RIGHT),tankG_image)
        tankB = Tank(200,500,0,(K_w,K_s,K_a,K_d),tankB_image)
        menu = "game"
```

A game over screen has already been blitted when the menu gets set to "dead". In Flycatcher we blitted the game over screen from inside the **menu == "dead"** statement but here, because we have two different ways for the game finishing, i.e. Blue wining or Green winning, then it makes sense to blit the game over screen from the places where the winner is declared.

Once in the **menu == "dead"** section, we've put in some mouse click detection for the section of the game over images that have the restart button, just like we did for the start menu. Should that mouse click get detected some conditions for the game need to be reset. Here we reset the shell list, after all there maybe shells still sitting in that list, and the tanks return to their original positions and directions. We don't need to reset **lives** because this is done in the Tank class's __init__().

SO YOU'RE SAYING WE MIGHT HAVE DONE
THINGS TOGETHER WE DON'T EVEN KNOW
ABOUT? YEAH. MAYBE A LOT OF THINGS.

280

Ammunition

We have a basic game. Let's add in a feature to make it a little more interesting. We're going to force the tanks to resupply from an ammunition dump. We're going to make it so the tanks can carry a maximum of ten shells. Then there will be two supply points where they can restock.

A player's shells will be displayed at the top of the screen so they know how many they have left. Like this:

Our Ammobox where we resupply with shells looks like this:

First let's add the images into the usual place in the set up part of the program. We've created an image called shell.png that we'll use to signify how many shells you have left as mentioned above. The image is just a single shell. We also have an image called ammobox.png that will be the icon for the ammunition dump.

```
shell_image = pygame.image.load("images/shell.png").convert_alpha()
ammobox_image = pygame.image.load("images/ammobox.png").convert_alpha()
```

```
Mike and Martha look deep into each other's eyes.
They move closer, their heartbeats quickening.
```

We're going build a class for our ammo box:

```
class Ammobox:
    def __init__(self,x,y):
        self.x = x
        self.y = y

    def draw(self):
        screen.blit(ammobox_image,(self.x,self.y))
```

We can see our basic class is quite simple. The __init__() function takes the position in which we're going place an ammo box, which will be given where the ammo boxes are created. We then have a draw() function to blit the image onto the screen.

We'll then create a list with the Ammobox constructors inside:

```
ammoboxes = (Ammobox(740,500),Ammobox(200,20))
```

We've created two ammo boxes and given them values for **x** and **y**.

Then we need to call the draw() function from the game loop. We're going to place a for loop after the for loop that controls the walls.

```
for ammobox in ammoboxes:
    ammobox.draw()
```

Now when we run the program we should see two ammo boxes placed at the coordinates given to the items in the list.

Mike touches Martha's hand. Her heart beats faster.

We need to add in some collision detection between the tanks and the ammo boxes. We'll create a new function called **collect()** into the Ammobox class to do this. We'll also make it so the ammo boxes disappear for ten seconds when hit by a tank. Let's write all this in at once.

```python
class Ammobox:
    def __init__(self,x,y):
        self.x = x
        self.y = y
        self.reappear = 0

    def collect(self,tank):
        if time.time() > self.reappear
                and pygame.Rect((self.x,self.y),ammobox_image.get_size())
                .colliderect((tank.x,tank.y+10),(60,60)):
            self.reappear = time.time() + 10

    def draw(self):
        if time.time() > self.reappear:
            screen.blit(ammobox_image,(self.x,self.y))
```

The **collect()** function detects collisions between an ammo box and a tank. Note that this function takes an argument, a tank. So a tank has to be fed to the function when it's called (page 284).

The line beginning "if" asks if time.time() is greater than self.reappear **and** if the tank fed to the function is colliding with the ammo box. At first time.time() is going to be bigger that **self.reappear** because **self.reappear** is zero. The Rect is placed at the coordinates of the ammo box (**self.x** and **self.y**) and is the same size as the ammo box (**ammobox_image.get_size()**). We then ask if the **Rect** collides with a second rectangle in **colliderect()**. This has the coordinates and size of the part of the tank we want to count in collisions (page 269).

If all this returns a True then **self.reappear** is set to **time.time() + 10**. This means the first condition of the if statement won't return another True for at least ten seconds. So for ten seconds the ammobox can't be collided with.

The draw() function will only blit the ammo box if time.time() is greater than self.reappear. So for ten seconds after a collision the ammo box won't be blitted.

We then need to call the **collect()** function from the for loop controlling the ammoboxes.

```
for ammobox in ammoboxes:
    ammobox.draw()
    ammobox.collect(tankG)
    ammobox.collect(tankB)
```

Here we're going through each ammobox in turn, calling the draw() function and then calling the collect() function for each tank.

If, instead of having two separate tanks we had a list of tanks, then the code would look like this:

```
for ammobox in ammoboxes:
    ammobox.draw()
    for tank in tanks:
        ammobox.collect(tank)
```

Here we have a for loop inside a for loop. Back on page 99 we used a while loop inside a while loop, but we haven't had to use a for loop inside a for loop in this book. It is, however, a commonly used technique. If you had a two lists and you wanted to detect collisions, or any interaction, between all the items on one list with all the items on the second, but you didn't need to delete those items, this is how you would do it.

HI GUYS. WOTCHA DOING? DO YOU WANT
TO BE PART OF MY NEW START UP?
YOU'LL GET STOCK OPTIONS.

We need to add in code to reduce the ammunition when we fire, and resupply when we collect an ammo box. We'll need an ammo variable. Add the following line into the Tank class's __init__() function:

```
self.ammo = 5
```

Then we add in a couple of lines to the fire() function:

```
def fire(self):
    if self.ammo > 0:
        shells.append(Shell(self.x+self.img.get_width()/2,
                        self.y+self.img.get_height()/2,self.dir))
        self.ammo -= 1
```

We can see that shells are only created when **self.ammo** is greater than zero, and that **self.ammo** reduces by one every time a shell is created.

Now we need to increase the number of shells when a tank hits an ammo box. An ammo box is going to be worth 5 shells and we're not allowed to carry more than ten shells at once. These changes are made in the Ammobox class's **collect()** function because that's where collisions between a tank and an ammobox are detected:

```
def collect(self,tank):
    if time.time() > self.reappear
            and pygame.Rect((self.x,self.y),box_image.get_size())
            .colliderect((tank.x,tank.y+10),(60,60)):
        tank.ammo = min(tank.ammo+5,10)
        self.reappear = time.time() + 10
```

The **min()** function takes the lowest value from its arguments. In this way we're setting the maximum value for ammo at 10. If you resupply when tank.ammo equals 3 you will leave with 8 shells. If you resupply when you all ready have 8 shells, you'll leave with 10.

At the moment the ammoboxes list (tuple really) isn't resetting when we restart the game so we need to do that in the restart code:

```
if menu == "dead":
    if pygame.mouse.get_pressed()[0] and
            pygame.Rect((555,444),(333,88)).collidepoint(pygame.mouse.get_pos()):
        shells = []
        tankG = Tank(740,20,180,(K_UP,K_DOWN,K_LEFT,K_RIGHT),tankG_image)
        tankB = Tank(200,500,0,(K_w,K_s,K_a,K_d),tankB_image)
        ammoboxes = (Ammobox(740,500),Ammobox(200,20))
        menu = "game"
```

We don't need to reset **ammo** because that's done in the Tank's __init__() function.

We do need to draw our shell icons onto the screen.

```
for i in range(tankG.ammo):
    screen.blit(shell_image,(987-i*10,5))

for i in range(tankB.ammo):
    screen.blit(shell_image,(5+i*10,5))
```

We've put the shell icon blitting code directly after the equivalent lines that blit lives, towards the end of the game loop. You don't have to place them where we have. As long as they're indented correctly it doesn't matter very much so long as they're after the line where we screen blit the landscape.

tankG.ammo is a variable containing the number of shells tankG has. We've seen the **range()** function before, on page 43. **range()** creates a list from zero to whatever integer has been given as an argument minus 1. So if **tankG.ammo** is 3 then range() returns the values 0, 1 and 2. The for loop goes through that list giving **i** the value of each item on the list in turn. So **i** will be 0 then 1 then 2. Note: If tankG.ammo is zero then range() returns an empty list (technically a tuple that is created once and then discarded) and so the for loop does nothing.

Then we use the value of **i** to blit the shell image at the coordinate given as the second argument in the screen.blit() function. We use **i** to modify the coordinate so each shell gets blitted 10 pixels (10*i) further along the x-axis. The tankG shells are getting blitted from right to left and the tankB shells are getting blitted from left to right. If **tankG.ammo** is equal to 1 then **i** will be zero and shell_image will be blitted at (987,5). If **tankG.ammo** is equal to 2 then **i** will be 1 and shell_image will be blitted at (967,5).

The same technique could be used for lives if you'd prefer a line of hearts or some such rather than the circle divided into thirds that we have used. Like this:

```
for i in range(tankG.lives):
    screen.blit(heart_image,(987-i*20,30))
```

We would have to have a heart image. Here we're placing the heart images 20 pixels apart and at 30 on the y-axis.

We just have a few last things. For starters the tanks can drive off the screen. Let's make it so they can drive partially off the screen but not disappear completely. The tank's move() function seems the place to do this. We already have four if statements dealing with the four controls. Let's add the following four if statements after them.

```
        if self.x < -30:
            self.x = -30
        if self.x > 970:
            self.x = 970
        if self.y < -30:
            self.y = -30
        if self.y > 570:
            self.y = 570
```

Now it's like there's a barrier 30 pixels off the edge of the screen that the tank can't cross. This means the tanks can move partially off the screen but not completely off the screen.

Another feature we could add is having an ammobox location move once an ammobox has been collected. This prevents a tank simply sitting in one spot and collecting ammunition every ten seconds. It forces the tanks to move around the screen.

```
    def collect(self,tank):
        if time.time() > self.reappear and
        pygame.Rect((self.x,self.y),ammobox_image.get_size()).colliderect((tank.x,tank.y+10),(60,60)):
            tank.ammo = min(tank.ammo+5,10)
            self.reappear = time.time() + 10
            if self.y == 20:
                self.y = 500
            else:
                self.y = 20
```

In the Ammobox's collect function we've added lines that change an ammobox's y position after a tank collects that ammobox The y position can only ever be 20 or 500. If it's 20 it gets changed to 500. If it isn't 20 (ie: it's 500), it gets changed to 20.

We could carry on tweaking the game forever. (Or a few hours, at least.) Maybe we could make each tank move at a different speed. This would be easy. We would just add a speed argument when we create the tanks and feed it into the Tank class's __init__() function. We'd make self.speed = speed. Then multiply dx and dy by speed. We could do the same with shell speed, adding a shell speed argument when a shell is created. The Shell class would then take the extra argument that would be used to dictate the shell's speed. So you maybe have a slow tank with faster shells. Or maybe we could give slower tanks more lives. The process would be pretty much the same. Add a lives argument when the tanks are created and make lives equal to that in the __init__() function. Of course this would mean changing the lives images, maybe using the row of hearts, or circles divided into different fractions.

But we have to stop somewhere. You, however can carry on.

And that's it. Four games and a lot of stuff learned. You should be comfortable now using classes, functions, loops, variables and many other things. You have the basic building blocks to make a hundred different games or to add a hundred new features to the games you've already made. Use your imagination.

We're going to start working on a second book that will expand on the themes of this book. We'll be focusing on platformer games. Meanwhile, keep experimenting and learn patience. There are many helpful websites and books, and there are coding clubs all over the world. Join one or start one if you can. If not, don't worry. All you really need is a computer and some perseverance. The lessons you learn best are the ones you teach yourself.

Good luck.

Index

General index

We have only indexed the page where an item is given a description.

Python functions

abs() 151
append() 9
int() 130
len() 46
math.atan2() 155
math.sin() 139
math.cos() 139
random.choice() 80
random.randint() 29
sys.exit() 9
time.time() 63

Pygame functions

collidepoint() 55
colliderect() 132
convert() 62
convert_alpha() 123
display.set_mode() 7
display.set_caption() 24
display.update() 15
draw.circle() 14
draw.line() 28
draw.rect() 15
event.get() 9
get_height() 148
get_width() 146
get_size() 133
image.load() 62
init() 6
key.get_pressed() 20
Mixer.init() 272
render() 104
screen.blit()
screen.fill((255,0,0)) 12
set_colorkey() 86
tick() 24
transform.rotate() 187
transform.rotozoom() 239

Functions and classes that we built.

Appendices

```python
import pygame, sys, time, random, time
from pygame.locals import *
pygame.init()
pygame.display.set_caption("rain")
screen = pygame.display.set_mode((1000,600))
clock = pygame.time.Clock()
mike_umbrella_image = pygame.image.load("images/Mike_umbrella.png").convert()
cloud_image = pygame.image.load("images/cloud.png").convert()
mike_image = pygame.image.load("images/Mike.png").convert()
last_hit_time = 0
raindrop_spawn_time=0

class Raindrop:
    def __init__(self, x,y):
        self.x = x
        self.y = y
        self.speed = random.randint(5,18)

    def move(self):
        self.y += self.speed

    def off_screen(self):
        return self.y > 800

    def draw(self):
        pygame.draw.line(screen,(0,0,0),(self.x,self.y),(self.x,self.y+5),1)

class Mike:
    def __init__(self):
        self.x = 300
        self.y = 390

    def hit_by(self,raindrop):
        return pygame.Rect(self.x,self.y,170,192).collidepoint((raindrop.x,raindrop.y))

    def draw(self):
        if time.time() > last_hit_time + 1:
            screen.blit(mike_image,(self.x,self.y))
        else:
            screen.blit(mike_umbrella_image,(self.x,self.y))

class Cloud:
    def __init__(self):
        self.x = 300
        self.y = 50

    def rain(self):
        for i in range(10):
            raindrops.append(Raindrop(random.randint(self.x,self.x+300),self.y+100))

    def move(self):
        if pressed_keys[K_RIGHT]:
            self.x+=1
        if pressed_keys[K_LEFT]:
            self.x-=1

    def draw(self):
        screen.blit(cloud_image,(self.x,self.y))

raindrops = []
mike = Mike()
cloud = Cloud()
```

```
while 1:
    clock.tick(60)
    for event in pygame.event.get():
        if event.type == QUIT:
            sys.exit()
    pressed_keys = pygame.key.get_pressed()

    screen.fill((255,255,255))

    mike.draw()

    cloud.draw()
    cloud.rain()
    cloud.move()

    i=0
    while i < len(raindrops):
        raindrops[i].move()
        raindrops[i].draw()
        flag = False
        if raindrops[i].off_screen():
            flag = True
        if mike.hit_by(raindrops[i]):
            flag = True
            last_hit_time = time.time()
        if flag:
            del raindrops[i]
            i-=1
        i+=1

    pygame.display.update()
```

```python
import pygame, sys, random, time
from pygame.locals import *
pygame.init()
clock = pygame.time.Clock()
pygame.display.set_caption("Space Invaders")
screen = pygame.display.set_mode((640,650))
badguy_image = pygame.image.load("images/badguy.png").convert()
badguy_image.set_colorkey((0,0,0))
fighter_image = pygame.image.load("images/fighter.png").convert()
fighter_image.set_colorkey((255,255,255))
GAME_OVER = pygame.image.load("images/gameover.png").convert()
font = pygame.font.Font(None,20)
last_badguy_spawn_time = 0
score = 0
shots = 0
hits = 0
misses = 0

class Badguy:
    def __init__(self):
        self.x = random.randint(0,520)
        self.y = -100
        self.dy = random.randint(2,6)
        self.dx = random.choice((-1,1))*self.dy

    def move(self):
        self.x += self.dx
        self.y += self.dy

    def bounce(self):
        if self.x < 0 or self.x > 570:
            self.dx *= -1

    def off_screen(self):
        return self.y > 640

    def touching(self,missile):
        return (self.x+35-missile.x)**2+(self.y+22-missile.y)**2 < 1225

    def score(self):
        global score
        score+=100

    def draw(self):
        screen.blit(badguy_image,(self.x,self.y))

class Fighter:
    def __init__(self):
        self.x = 320

    def move(self):
        if pressed_keys[K_LEFT] and self.x > 0:
            self.x -=3
        if pressed_keys[K_RIGHT] and self.x < 540:
            self.x +=3

    def fire(self):
        global shots
        shots+=1
        missiles.append(Missile(self.x+50))

    def hit_by(self,badguy):
        return (
                badguy.y > 546 and
                badguy.x > self.x - 70 and
                badguy.x < self.x + 100
                )

    def draw(self):
        screen.blit(fighter_image,(self.x,591))

class Missile:
    def __init__(self,x):
        self.x = x
        self.y = 591

    def move(self):
        self.y -= 5

    def off_screen(self):
        return self.y < -8

    def draw(self):
        pygame.draw.line(screen,(255,0,0),(self.x,self.y),(self.x,self.y+8),1)

badguys = []
fighter = Fighter()
missiles = []
```

```
while 1:
    clock.tick(60)
    for event in pygame.event.get():
        if event.type == QUIT:
            sys.exit()
        if event.type == KEYDOWN and event.key == K_SPACE:
            fighter.fire()
    pressed_keys = pygame.key.get_pressed()
    if time.time() - last_badguy_spawn_time > 0.5:
        badguys.append(Badguy())
        last_badguy_spawn_time = time.time()

    screen.fill((0,0,0))
    fighter.move()
    fighter.draw()

    i = 0
    while i < len(badguys):
        badguys[i].move()
        badguys[i].bounce()
        badguys[i].draw()
        if badguys[i].off_screen():
            del badguys[i]
            i -= 1
        i += 1

    i = 0
    while i < len(missiles):
        missiles[i].move()
        missiles[i].draw()
        if missiles[i].off_screen():
            del missiles[i]
            misses += 1
            i -= 1
        i += 1

    i = 0
    while i < len(badguys):
        j = 0
        while j < len(missiles):
            if badguys[i].touching(missiles[j]):
                badguys[i].score()
                hits += 1
                del badguys[i]
                del missiles[j]
                i -= 1
                break
            j += 1
        i += 1

    screen.blit(font.render("Score: "+str(score),True,(255,255,255)),(5,5))

    for badguy in badguys:
        if fighter.hit_by(badguy):
            screen.blit(GAME_OVER,(170,200))

            screen.blit(font.render(str(shots),True,(255,255,255)),(266,320))
            screen.blit(font.render(str(score),True,(255,255,255)),(266,348))
            screen.blit(font.render(str(hits),True,(255,255,255)),(400,320))
            screen.blit(font.render(str(misses),True,(255,255,255)),(400,337))
            if shots == 0:
                screen.blit(font.render("--",True,(255,255,255)),(400,357))
            else:
                screen.blit(font.render(str((1000*hits/shots)/10.)+"%",True,(255,
255,255)),(400,357))
            while 1:
                for event in pygame.event.get():
                    if event.type == QUIT:
                        sys.exit()
                pygame.display.update()

    pygame.display.update()
```

```
import pygame, sys, math, random, time
from pygame.locals import *
pygame.init()
pygame.display.set_caption("Pong")
screen = pygame.display.set_mode((1000,600))
clock = pygame.time.Clock()
ball_image = pygame.image.load("images/ball.png").convert_alpha()
rscore = 0
lscore = 0
font = pygame.font.Font(None,40)
font2 = pygame.font.SysFont("corbel",70)
font3 = pygame.font.Font(None,60)
font4 = pygame.font.Font(None,30)
match_start = time.time()

class Bat:
    def __init__(self,ctrls,x,side):
        self.ctrls=ctrls
        self.x=x
        self.y=260
        self.side=side
        self.lastbop = 0

    def move(self):
        if pressed_keys[self.ctrls[0]] and self.y > 0:
            self.y -= 10
        if pressed_keys[self.ctrls[1]] and self.y < 520:
            self.y += 10

    def bop(self):
        if time.time() > self.lastbop + 0.3:
            self.lastbop = time.time()

    def draw(self):
        offset = -self.side*(time.time() < self.lastbop+0.05)*10
        pygame.draw.line(screen,(255,255,255),(self.x+offset,self.y),(self.x+offset,self.y+80),6)

class Ball:
    def __init__(self):
        self.d=((math.pi/3)*random.random()+(math.pi/3))+math.pi*random.randint(0,1)
        self.speed = 12
        self.dx=math.sin(self.d)*self.speed
        self.dy=math.cos(self.d)*self.speed
        self.x=475
        self.y=275

    def move(self):
        self.x +=self.dx
        self.y +=self.dy

    def bounce(self):
        if (self.y<=0 and self.dy < 0) or (self.y>=550 and self.dy > 0):
            self.dy *=-1
            self.d = math.atan2(self.dx,self.dy)

        for bat in bats:
            if pygame.Rect(bat.x,bat.y,6,80).colliderect(self.x,self.y,50,50) and abs(self.dx)/self.dx == bat.side:
                self.d += random.random()*math.pi/4 -math.pi/8

                if (0 < self.d < math.pi/6) or (math.pi*5/6 < self.d < math.pi):
                    self.d=((math.pi/3)*random.random()+(math.pi/3))
                elif (math.pi < self.d < math.pi*7/6) or (math.pi*11/6 < self.d < math.pi*2):
                    self.d=((math.pi/3)*random.random()+(math.pi/3))+math.pi

                self.d *= -1
                self.d%=math.pi*2

                if time.time() < bat.lastbop + 0.05 and self.speed < 20:
                    self.speed *= 1.5

                self.dx=math.sin(self.d)*self.speed
                self.dy=math.cos(self.d)*self.speed

    def draw(self):
        screen.blit(ball_image,(self.x, self.y))

ball = Ball()
bats = [ Bat( [K_a,K_z] , 10,-1), Bat( [K_UP,K_DOWN] , 984,1) ]
```

```
while 1:
    clock.tick(30)
    for event in pygame.event.get():
        if event.type == QUIT:
            sys.exit()
        if event.type == KEYDOWN:
            if event.key == K_q:
                bats[0].bop()
            if event.key == K_RSHIFT:
                bats[1].bop()
    pressed_keys = pygame.key.get_pressed()

    screen.fill((0,0,0))

    pygame.draw.line(screen,(255,255,255),(screen.get_width()/2,50),(screen.get_width()/2,screen.get_height()),3)
    pygame.draw.circle(screen,(255,255,255),(screen.get_width()/2, screen.get_height()/2),50,3)

    for bat in bats:
        bat.move()
        bat.draw()

    if ball.x < -50:
        ball=Ball()
        rscore+=1

    if ball.x > 1000:
        ball=Ball()
        lscore+=1

    txt = font.render(str(lscore),True,(255,255,255))
    screen.blit(txt,(20,20))
    txt = font.render(str(rscore),True,(255,255,255))
    screen.blit(txt,(980-txt.get_width(),20))

    txt = font.render(str(int(time.time() - match_start)),True,(255,255,255))
    screen.blit(txt,(screen.get_width()/2 -txt.get_width()/2,20))

    if time.time()- match_start > 60:

        txt = font2.render("score",True,(255,0,255))
        screen.blit(txt,(screen.get_width()/4 - txt.get_width()/2, screen.get_height()/4))
        screen.blit(txt,(screen.get_width()*3/4 - txt.get_width()/2, screen.get_height()/4))
        txt = font3.render(str(lscore),True,(255,255,255))
        screen.blit(txt,(screen.get_width()/4 - txt.get_width()/2,screen.get_height()/2))
        txt = font3.render(str(rscore),True,(255,255,255))
        screen.blit(txt,(screen.get_width()*3/4 - txt.get_width()/2, screen.get_height()/2))
        txt = font4.render("Press Space to restart",True,(255,255,255))
        screen.blit(txt,(screen.get_width()*5/9,screen.get_height()-50))

        while 1:
            for event in pygame.event.get():
                if event.type == QUIT:
                    sys.exit()
            pressed_keys = pygame.key.get_pressed()

            if pressed_keys[K_SPACE]:
                lscore = 0
                rscore = 0
                bats[0].y = 200
                bats[1].y = 200
                match_start = time.time()
                ball = Ball()
                break
            pygame.display.update()

    ball.move()
    ball.draw()
    ball.bounce()

    pygame.display.update()
```

```
import pygame, sys, time, random, math
from pygame.locals import *
pygame.init()
clock = pygame.time.Clock()
screen = pygame.display.set_mode((1000,600))
fly_image = pygame.image.load("images/fly.png").convert_alpha()
frog_image = pygame.image.load("images/frog.png").convert_alpha()
homescreen_image = pygame.image.load("images/flycatcher_home.png").convert_alpha()
gameover_image = pygame.image.load("images/flycatcher_game_over.png").convert_alpha()
fly_sound = pygame.mixer.Sound("sounds/fly-buzz.ogg")
tongue_sound = pygame.mixer.Sound("sounds/tongue.ogg")
font = pygame.font.SysFont("draglinebtndm",60)
font2 = pygame.font.SysFont("couriernew",15)
menu = "start"
death_time = False

class Fly:
    def __init__(self):
        self.x = random.randint(0,screen.get_width()-fly_image.get_width())
        self.y = random.randint(0,screen.get_height()-fly_image.get_height())
        self.dir = random.randint(0,359)
        self.spawn_time = time.time()
        fly_sound.play()
        self.stuck = False

    def draw(self):
        if self.stuck:
            tpos = frog.get_tongue_pos()
            screen.blit(fly_image, (tpos[0]-fly_image.get_width()/2, tpos[1]-fly_image.get_height()/2))
        elif time.time() > self.spawn_time + 1.4 and time.time() < self.spawn_time + 3.4:
            rotated = pygame.transform.rotate(fly_image,self.dir)
            screen.blit(rotated, (self.x,self.y))

    def stick(self):
        if not self.stuck and time.time() > self.spawn_time + 1.4 and time.time() < self.spawn_time + 3.4:
            tpos = frog.get_tongue_pos()
            fpos = (self.x+fly_image.get_width()/2,self.y+fly_image.get_height()/2)
            if (tpos[0]-fpos[0])**2+(tpos[1]-fpos[1])**2 < (fly_image.get_width()/2+10)**2:
                self.stuck = True

class Frog:
    def __init__(self):
        self.dir = 0
        self.tongue_dist = 0
        self.tongue_extend = 0
        self.energy = 100

    def move(self):
        self.tongue_dist += self.tongue_extend * 10
        if self.tongue_dist ** 2 > (fly.x-screen.get_width()/2)** 2 + (fly.y-screen.get_height()/2)** 2:
            self.tongue_extend = -1
        if self.tongue_dist == 0:
            self.tongue_extend = 0
            if pressed_keys[K_LEFT]:
                self.dir+=4
            if pressed_keys[K_RIGHT]:
                self.dir-=4

    def get_tongue_pos(self):
        return (
                int(screen.get_width()/2-self.tongue_dist*math.sin(math.radians(self.dir))),
                int(screen.get_height()/2-self.tongue_dist*math.cos(math.radians(self.dir)))
               )

    def tongue_poke(self):
        if self.tongue_dist == 0:
            self.tongue_extend = 1
            tongue_sound.play()

    def draw(self):

        if death_time:
            rotated = pygame.transform.rotozoom(frog_image,self.dir,1-((time.time()-death_time)/2))
            screen.blit(rotated, (screen.get_width()/2-rotated.get_width()/2,
            screen.get_height()/2-rotated.get_height()/2))
        else:
            tpos = self.get_tongue_pos()
            pygame.draw.circle(screen,(255,50,50),tpos,10)
            pygame.draw.line(screen,(255,50,50),(screen.get_width()/2,screen.get_height()/2),tpos,10)
            rotated = pygame.transform.rotate(frog_image,self.dir)
            screen.blit(rotated,(screen.get_width()/2-rotated.get_width()/2, screen.get_height()/2-rotated.get_height()/2))

fly = None
frog = Frog()
```

```
while 1:
    clock.tick(60)
    for event in pygame.event.get():
        if event.type == QUIT:
            sys.exit()
        if event.type == KEYDOWN and event.key == K_SPACE:
            frog.tongue_poke()
    pressed_keys = pygame.key.get_pressed()

    if menu == "start":
        screen.blit(homescreen_image,(0,0))
        txt = font.render("Play",True,(255,255,255))
        txt_x = 705
        txt_y = 435
        buttonrect = pygame.Rect((txt_x,txt_y),txt.get_size())
        pygame.draw.rect(screen,(200,50,0),buttonrect)
        screen.blit(txt, (txt_x, txt_y))

    if pygame.mouse.get_pressed()[0] and buttonrect.collidepoint(pygame.mouse.get_pos()):
        menu = "game"
        game_start = time.time()

    if menu == "game":

        frog.energy -= 0.1

        if fly == None or time.time() > fly.spawn_time + 4.4 and not fly.stuck:
            fly = Fly()

        if fly.stuck and frog.tongue_dist == 0:
            energy = min(100, frog.energy+50)
            fly = Fly()

        screen.fill((255,255,255))

        frog.move()
        frog.draw()
        fly.stick()
        fly.draw()

        if frog.energy >= 0:
            pygame.draw.rect(screen,(200,50,0),(10,110,20,-frog.energy))

        if frog.energy <= 0 and not death_time and frog.tongue_dist == 0:
            death_time = time.time()

        if death_time:
            txt = font.render("Time:"+str(int((death_time - game_start)*10)/10.),True,(0,0,0))
        else:
            txt = font2.render("Time:"+str(int((time.time()-game_start)*10)/10.),True,(0,0,0))
            screen.blit(txt,(10,120))

        if death_time and time.time() > death_time + 2:
            menu = "dead"

    if menu == "dead":
        screen.blit(gameover_image,(0,0))
        txt = font2.render("You survived: "+str(int((death_time - game_start)*10)/10.)+"seconds",True,(0,0,0))
        screen.blit(txt,(705,500))

        txt = font.render("Play",True,(255,255,255))
        txt_x = 705
        txt_y = 235
        buttonrect = pygame.Rect((txt_x,txt_y),txt.get_size())
        pygame.draw.rect(screen,(200,50,0),buttonrect)
        screen.blit(txt, (txt_x, txt_y))

        if pygame.mouse.get_pressed()[0] and buttonrect.collidepoint(pygame.mouse.get_pos()):
            menu = "game"
            game_start = time.time()
            frog.energy = 100
            death_time = False
            fly = None
            frog = Frog()

    pygame.display.update()
```

```python
import pygame, sys, time, random, math
from pygame.locals import *
pygame.mixer.init(buffer=512)
pygame.init()
pygame.display.set_caption("Tank Battle")
clock = pygame.time.Clock()
screen = pygame.display.set_mode((1000,600))
homescreen_image = pygame.image.load("images/TBhomescreen.jpg").convert()
landscape_image = pygame.image.load("images/landscape.jpg").convert()
wall_image = pygame.image.load("images/wall.png").convert()
vert_wall_image = pygame.transform.rotate(wall_image,90)
tankG_image = pygame.image.load("images/tankG.png").convert_alpha()
tankB_image = pygame.image.load("images/tankB.png").convert_alpha()
shell_sound = pygame.mixer.Sound("sounds/shell.ogg")
harm_sound = pygame.mixer.Sound("sounds/tank_hit.ogg")

G_lives=(
            pygame.image.load("images/lives_1G.png").convert_alpha(),
            pygame.image.load("images/lives_2G.png").convert_alpha(),
            pygame.image.load("images/lives_3G.png").convert_alpha()
        )
B_lives=(
            pygame.image.load("images/lives_1B.png").convert_alpha(),
            pygame.image.load("images/lives_2B.png").convert_alpha(),
            pygame.image.load("images/lives_3B.png").convert_alpha()
        )

G_wins = pygame.image.load("images/greenwins.jpg").convert()
B_wins = pygame.image.load("images/bluewins.jpg").convert()
shell_image = pygame.image.load("images/shell.png").convert_alpha()
ammobox_image = pygame.image.load("images/ammobox.png").convert_alpha()
menu = "home"

class Wall:
    def __init__(self,x,y,vert):
        self.x = x
        self.y = y
        self.vert = vert
        self.speed = 1

    def draw(self):
        if self.vert:
            screen.blit(vert_wall_image,(self.x,self.y))
        else:
            screen.blit(wall_image,(self.x,self.y))

    def move(self):
        if self.vert:
            self.y+=self.speed
        else:
            self.x+=self.speed

        if (
            (self.vert and (self.y < 50 or self.y > 350)) or
            (not self.vert and ((self.x < 50 or self.x > 750) or (self.x > 200 and self.x <600))):
            )
            self.speed*=-1

class Tank:
    def __init__(self,x,y,dir,ctrls,img):
        self.x = x
        self.y = y
        self.ctrls = ctrls
        self.dir = dir
        self.img = img
        self.flash_time_end = 0
        self.lives = 3
        self.ammo = 5
```

```
    def move(self):
        dx = math.sin(math.radians(self.dir))
        dy = math.cos(math.radians(self.dir))
        if pressed_keys[self.ctrls[0]]:
            self.x-=dx
            self.y-=dy
        if pressed_keys[self.ctrls[1]]:
            self.x+=0.5*dx
            self.y+=0.5*dy
        if pressed_keys[self.ctrls[2]]:
            self.dir+=1
        if pressed_keys[self.ctrls[3]]:
            self.dir-=1
        if self.x < -30:
            self.x = -30
        if self.x > 970:
            self.x = 970
        if self.y < -30:
            self.y = -30
        if self.y > 570:
            self.y = 570

    def fire(self):
        if self.ammo > 0:
            shells.append(Shell(self.x+self.img.get_width()/2,self.y+self.img.get_height()/2,self.dir))
            self.ammo -= 1

    def hit_shell(self,shell):
        return pygame.Rect(self.x,self.y+10,60,60).collidepoint(shell.x,shell.y)

    def harm(self):
        if time.time() > self.flash_time_end:
            self.flash_time_end = time.time() + 2
            self.lives -= 1

    def hit_wall(self,wall):
        return (
            (wall.vert and pygame.Rect((wall.x,wall.y),vert_wall_image.get_size()).colliderect((self.x,self.y+10),(60,60)))or
            (not wall.vert and pygame.Rect((wall.x,wall.y),wall_image.get_size()).colliderect((self.x,self.y+10),(60,60)))
            )

    def draw(self):
        if time.time() > self.flash_time_end or time.time() % 0.1 < 0.05:
            rotated = pygame.transform.rotate(self.img,self.dir)
            screen.blit(
                    rotated,(self.x+self.img.get_width()/2-rotated.get_width()/2,
                        self.y+self.img.get_height()/2-rotated.get_height()/2)
                    )

class Shell:
    def __init__(self,x,y,dir):
        self.dx = -math.sin(math.radians(dir))*5
        self.dy = -math.cos(math.radians(dir))*5
        self.x = x + self.dx * 8
        self.y = y + self.dy * 8
        self.bounces = 0
        shell_sound.play()

    def move(self):
        self.x += self.dx
        self.y += self.dy

    def draw(self):
        pygame.draw.circle(screen, (100,50,50), (int(self.x), int(self.y)), 3)

    def bounce(self):
        for wall in walls:
            if wall.vert and pygame.Rect((wall.x,wall.y),
                    vert_wall_image.get_size()).collidepoint(self.x,self.y):
                self.dx*=-1
                self.bounces += 1

            if not wall.vert and pygame.Rect((wall.x,wall.y),
                    wall_image.get_size()).collidepoint(self.x,self.y):
                self.dy*=-1
                self.bounces += 1

        if self.x < 0 or self.x > 1000:
            self.dx*=-1
            self.bounces += 1

        if self.y < 0 or self.y > 600:
            self.dy*=-1
            self.bounces += 1
```

Continues on following page

```
class Ammobox:
    def __init__(self,x,y):
        self.x = x
        self.y = y
        self.reappear = 0

    def collect(self,tank):
        if time.time() > self.reappear and
⏎              pygame.Rect((self.x,self.y),ammobox_image.get_size()).colliderect((tank.x,tank.y+10),(60,60)):
            tank.ammo = min(tank.ammo+5,10)
            self.reappear = time.time() + 10
            if self.y == 20:
                self.y = 500
            else:
                self.y = 20
    def draw(self):
        if time.time() > self.reappear:
            screen.blit(ammobox_image,(self.x,self.y))


walls = (Wall(496,200,True),Wall(50,150,False),Wall(600,150,False), Wall(50,435,False),Wall(600,435,False))
tankG = Tank(740,20,180,(K_UP,K_DOWN,K_LEFT,K_RIGHT),tankG_image)
tankB = Tank(200,500,0,(K_w,K_s,K_a,K_d),tankB_image)
shells = []
ammoboxes = (Ammobox(740,500),Ammobox(200,20))

while 1:
    clock.tick(60)

    for event in pygame.event.get():
        if event.type == QUIT:
            sys.exit()
        if event.type == KEYDOWN and event.key == K_RSHIFT and menu == "game":
            tankG.fire()
        if event.type == KEYDOWN and event.key == K_q and menu == "game":
            tankB.fire()
    pressed_keys = pygame.key.get_pressed()

    if menu == "home":
        screen.blit(homescreen_image,(0,0))
        buttonrect = pygame.Rect(409,440,147,147)
        if pygame.mouse.get_pressed()[0] and buttonrect.collidepoint(pygame.mouse.get_pos()):
            menu = "game"

    if menu == "game":
        tankG.move()
        tankB.move()

        screen.blit(landscape_image,(0,0))

        tankG.draw()
        tankB.draw()

        for wall in walls:
            wall.move()
            wall.draw()

            if tankG.hit_wall(wall):
                tankG.harm()

            if tankB.hit_wall(wall):
                tankB.harm()

        for ammobox in ammoboxes:
            ammobox.draw()
            ammobox.collect(tankG)
            ammobox.collect(tankB)
```

```
        i = 0
        while i < len(shells):
            shells[i].move()
            shells[i].bounce()
            shells[i].draw()
            flag = False

            if tankG.hit_shell(shells[i]):
                tankG.harm()
                harm_sound.play()
                flag = True

            if tankB.hit_shell(shells[i]):
                tankB.harm()
                harm_sound.play()
                flag = True

            if shells[i].bounces == 5:
                flag = True

            if flag:
                del shells[i]
                i -= 1
            i+=1

        screen.blit(G_lives[tankG.lives-1],(965,30))
        screen.blit(B_lives[tankB.lives-1],(5,30))

        for i in range(tankG.ammo):
            screen.blit(shell_image,(987-i*10,5))

        for i in range(tankB.ammo):
            screen.blit(shell_image,(5+i*10,5))

        if tankG.lives == 0:
            screen.blit(B_wins,(0,0))
            menu = "dead"

        if tankB.lives == 0:
            screen.blit(G_wins,(0,0))
            menu = "dead"

if menu == "dead":
    if pygame.mouse.get_pressed()[0] and pygame.Rect((555,444),(333,88)).collidepoint(pygame.mouse.get_pos()):
        shells = []
        tankG = Tank(740,20,180,(K_UP,K_DOWN,K_LEFT,K_RIGHT),tankG_image)
        tankB = Tank(200,500,0,(K_w,K_s,K_a,K_d),tankB_image)
        ammoboxes = (Ammobox(740,500),Ammobox(200,20))
        menu = "game"
pygame.display.update()
```

20775793R00185

Printed in Poland
by Amazon Fulfillment
Poland Sp. z o.o., Wrocław